composed sea, separately and together, remained a mystery, incomprehensible. Any thoughts on such a weighty matter seemed to be obscured by the asphalt, the footpaths, the houses, traffic, powerlines and family nearby. Still he is facing the camera and vaguely aware of himself, conscious of his presence on this patch of earth, named Adelaide, which always felt to be a great distance from anywhere else. For his mother religion did its best to fill in the gaps. It was makeshift, and perhaps was a help to her.

He.

ALSO BY MURRAY BAIL

The Drover's Wife and Other Stories
Homesickness
Holden's Performance
Eucalyptus
Camouflage
The Pages
The Voyage

Notebooks 1970–2003
Fairweather

Murray Bail

He.

Text Publishing Melbourne Australia

textpublishing.com.au

The Text Publishing Company
Swann House, 22 William Street, Melbourne Victoria 3000,
Australia

A part of this work appeared in slightly different form in the *Monthly* magazine.

Published by The Text Publishing Company, 2021

Book design by Chong W.H.

Printed and bound in Australia by Griffin Press, part of Ovato, an accredited ISO/NZS 14001:2004 Environmental Management System printer.

ISBN: 9781922330949 (hardback)

ISBN: 9781922459060 (ebook)

A catalogue record for this book is available from the National Library of Australia.

This book is printed on paper certified against the Forest Stewardship Council® Standards. Griffin Press holds FSC chain-of-custody certification SGS-COC-005088. FSC promotes environmentally responsible, socially beneficial and economically viable management of the world's forests.

We lose track of everything, and of everyone, even ourselves. —*Marguerite Yourcenar*

He.

And in the middle in khaki shorts, dusty knees, is he. Aged twelve he already has a certain earnestness, the solemnity, trying to comprehend what is incomprehensible, 'he wouldn't know what day it is'. Finding a reason for what existed around him, at arm's length and behind and everywhere else, including places he could not see, and the immensity of the sky above and the loosely composed sea, separately and together, remained a mystery, incomprehensible. Any thoughts on such a weighty matter seemed to be obscured by the asphalt, the footpaths, the houses, traffic, power-lines and family nearby. Still he is facing the camera and vaguely aware of himself, conscious of his presence on this patch of earth, named Adelaide, which always felt to be a great distance from anywhere else. For his mother, religion did its best to fill in the gaps. It was makeshift, and perhaps was a help to her.

Next to him, his two brothers and sister. They have long since retired from work, occupied with hobbies and grandchildren and staying healthy, not always in that order. His mother and father are no longer alive. All his aunts and uncles have died. Mothers- and fathers-in-law are no more. All dead. And Mr Townsend, the grocer, in his apron, the black hair combed like a perfectly ploughed paddock, announcing himself at the back door, 'Gro-cer!' and walking straight into the kitchen, the milkman and his horse too, long dead, as is the man who delivered the bread from a glossy green cart pulled by a horse. Mr Hedley, the watchmaker in the next street, thin man with a large, freckled wife, smoked a cigarette on the tram to work, nicotine stains on the fingers of one hand; no longer alive. They no longer exist. Even in memory they have become insubstantial, barely recognisable. Having once been seen, they remain part of his life. As almost-remembered.

With his father standing on the wall looking at the fiery sunset, 'Is that the war?'

There was the good ship Venus / By Christ you should have seen us…

And other schoolboy ditties, mostly to do with hopeless curiosity.

Lady of Spain, I adore you, pull down your pants and I'll explore you.

Large spider that came out of the tap of the tank outside the laundry as he bent forward to take a drink.

Those sharp-edged, pale brown sandhills repeated to infinity in the Sahara. The cleanliness of the desert, unearthly.

The black skin the colour of sump oil of the Tuareg wrapped in scarves who'd come in to Timbuktu, leading seventy camels from the salt mine at Touerat, each camel laden with rectangular slabs of pale brown salt. Perhaps in his fifties, it was hard to tell. A calm, level gaze with bloodshot eyes, and he was coughing, ill with tuberculosis.

His tremendous stoicism out of necessity.

Twenty or thirty pigeons took off from the date palm in the Stewarts' front garden halfway along the street, flying back and forth with mathematical precision, abruptly changing direction in unison, zigzagging en masse for no apparent reason. 'There has to be a leader,' his father gave them a glance.

The pigeons flew in formation on many days, then they were gone.

The street called Galway Grove, short street, parallel to the Adelaide Hills, the house number 11 halfway along. It had a small verandah painted red that nobody used. He couldn't recall anybody ever sitting on the verandah. Every house had a front hedge of some kind. There were trees along the footpath. Nearby streets had been given the names of English poets, Shelley Street, Dryden Street, Milton Avenue, Tennyson Avenue, and the longest and broadest of them all, Shakespeare Avenue. It would not have been at all possible to have a Dante Avenue or Goethe Street.

People drank tea and avoided eating in public places, such as on pavements.

At one end, forming a T, was another street and a house hidden by an unruly hedge. Nobody could remember the hedge ever being cut. Cast in darkness the house gave off a feeling of dread. He and his friends didn't dare to open the gate to have a look in case they were caught. Robbers, a murderer with an axe, or an angry madwoman could have lived there. Whoever it was did not want to be seen, nor care about the condition of their hedge. The garden was a mess too. Occasionally a faint light could be seen, so somebody was there, which only made it worse. In full view directly opposite was a two-storey house, not with a corrugated-iron roof like his, but of orange tiles. A two-storey house: in his suburb hardly any. Mr Treloar, a wheat broker, owned the tiled house. He had two sons and a daughter, who went to private schools. A short man with a florid face he seemed to breathe through his teeth. He wore bow ties. Certainly was the most sardonic man he had met at that stage. His wife was a handsome woman, unnecessarily imperious, who endowed her daughter with the large breasts. Next door was a bungalow set back, the city base for the owners of "Collinsville", the world-famous fine-wool stud somewhere north of Adelaide.

If people read novels they were English novels. The

Treloars lent him not Dickens, but Thackeray, Maugham, Kipling and Hardy. It was as if the big houses had the books, not entirely untrue. And he ended up reading most of Thomas Hardy's novels, at least all those the Treloars had in the house. Mr Treloar gave him a present of Hardy's short stories, *Life's Little Ironies*. Interesting title. The rural melancholy of Hardy was recognisable on the other side of the world, in dry Protestant Adelaide.

Two houses away in a hollow was Mr Fromain, the manager of an ice-cream factory. He had been an officer at Gallipoli; therefore, for his occasional visits to their teetotal house a single brown bottle of beer was bought and placed in the fridge, like a bomb, and in the lounge room his father offered a cigarette from a small barrel of ebony-black bakelite, the material used for wireless cabinets.

Old people who were only distantly related were called 'uncle' or 'aunt'. Uncle Frank lived in the suburb called Prospect with his sister, Em, who had an exceptionally long powdered face. She always wore an oval brooch. Their lavatory in the backyard like a wardrobe, near the back fence. Shell shock from the First World War had left Uncle Frank with a twisted mouth and slurred speech. He shaved with an open blade, the leather strop at the ready, as if he was still in the army. During visits he readily pulled out from the bottom of his wardrobe the Mauser pistol in its dark tan holster, which had the live bullets still clipped on the outside, captured from a German officer when Uncle Frank leapt into a trench. His bare, unadorned bedroom. Uncle Frank worked as a stonemason, making headstones at Tillett's on West Terrace.

Men who came back from being in battle were held in high regard, until Vietnam where the enemy was not really visible.

Crossing the creek bed in the Flinders Ranges as a wedge-tail eagle swooped and struck the roof of the car.

At intervals along the Suez Canal: eucalypts.

In Paris near rue de Seine from a third-floor window the woman throwing down a man's belongings onto the street.

Three young women in short skirts walking in a row laughing, near midnight, Kings Cross.

Elephants moving close by through the bush, without making a sound. Zimbabwe.

The photograph of Beckett at a restaurant in Paris laughing at something Patrick Magee has said, February 17, 1964.

'What school did you go to?'

Instead of 'Egypt' they said 'Egg-wiped'.

Two women weeping in front of the Anselm Kiefer paintings, St. Louis.

In the Southern Ocean before dawn when the sea angry and old casually tossed and rolled the enormous ship.

Afterwards, her face on the pillow was softened and smoothed. A smiling, mid-distant expression.

Water passed through the first floor of a wooden house pushing out the curtains, as if by a wind. The Mississippi in flood, St. Louis. It was 1993.

Many sunsets. They have turned into the one sunset.

The first readings of Musil, Proust, Trotsky, Borges, *Anna Karenina*; how the entire world expanded, and included him.

So many men at Mallala Air Force Base wore dark moustaches, in turn making them look false.

The heavy slop of water: Venice. The paintings of Canaletto, Turner, etc. didn't prepare him for it.

Those camels in northern India, others wandering left to right, North Africa.

The green of Cooper's Creek, a welcome line of colour in the desert.

Prisoner in chains being led along the street. Kabul, 1969.

'Just a minute, I'll put the kettle on.'
'I haven't got the faintest idea.'

'You never know what tomorrow's going to bring.'

Mid-morning in Perth the woman sitting alone in the parked car weeping, who turned when he offered help: 'Leave me! Go away!'

The stout tan shoes displayed in the tray of water in the window of Cordings on Piccadilly, demonstrating the waterproof qualities of these shoes. They remained in the window, even after a leak had emptied the tray of water.

On the back verandah, Barkly Street: the shadow of an airliner crossed the lawn, pointing like an arrow. About as large as a man it flowed over the fence and was gone.

His father never ate rabbit—the Depression years.

The piano tuner who came to the house carrying a small bag as if impersonating the local doctor.

Above the piano a framed print of Raeburn's painting of a boy with his hand around a white rabbit.

Walking across the room just in his underpants and dark socks reminded him of Bulgaria or the Soviet Union.

Woman on Macleay Street squatting at a side mirror of a parked car applying lipstick who looked up and smiled.

'If I may state the bleeding obvious…'

(My father's friends—I don't recall any.)

The locust plague, Adelaide. Grasshoppers? They were large and settled on clothes, faces and hair, on all the leaves, and on the streets, where they were squashed under the wheels of bikes and cars. Sometime between 1950 and 1952.

Taking the easy way and not actually telling the truth.

The fig tree in the backyard, to the right of the back door.

He never saw his parents naked, not even his father.

Masks are put on faded faces to save them.

He thought of war, not whether it was just or not, but how he would behave.

The sunset over the oasis in Morocco when everything was stationary.

He was told by older men that sleeping with a woman was 'the equivalent to a nine-mile walk'.

Nothing like it had happened in Adelaide before. A night in 1948, when he was seven, his father hurriedly took him and his older brother to Victoria Square where a fire was destroying the Moore's Department Store. Other children were also there in pyjamas and dressing gowns. While all eyes were fixed on the smoke and flames flowing from the windows of the stricken building he was looking down at the firemen struggling with their canvas hoses, which lay on the ground like pythons, leaking and spraying jets of water—yet when he looked up there was still enough water to reach the tall building.

After the Moore's fire a Jaguar two-seater sports car was acquired for the fire chief. It was painted bright red, and had a siren fitted on the front mudguard. Parked alongside the fire engines, the high-performance car was ready to screech off with the fire chief at the wheel to reach a fire well ahead of anybody else. Whenever their father was driving anywhere near the fire station he was screamed and yelled at to stop for a second so they could glimpse the red Jaguar lined up ready to go.

The heavy timber of the wharf, Port Adelaide. The splintered greyness which matched his father's face settled over the steering wheel on the Sunday afternoon drive. At a porthole a bearded blond face looked down as he looked up and tossed down a gift, a box of matches. He looked at it in his hand: *Made in Sweden*. How such a minor incident of giving can remain in memory.

Many years later those long voyages in container ships.

The small milk bar on Magill Road run by a man noticeable for his red nose and paunch, always the short-sleeve shirt, and his sister, who never smiled. There was a bell on the door, because they were never at the counter. He wondered what they were doing behind the curtain out the back. Mostly empty shelves. He'd pour the clotted cream from a large tin, an arthritic knuckle on his hand standing out like a golf ball. Mr Cruikshank and his sister. 'Go to Cruikshank's and get some cream.'

After the war .303 rifles were readily available in War Disposal stores, along with khaki water bottles, belts and army trousers, gas masks, goggles, boots and olive-green ammunition boxes. It was even possible to buy an aeroplane—no longer needed—and some men did, bought a Wirraway or an Avro Anson and stripped it in their backyard for the aluminium and copper. These could be glimpsed with their wings removed, like the unfinished boat being built on the front drive of other houses. He bought a .303 for five pounds and kept it in his wardrobe among his trousers, now and then going up into the hills and firing into the trees and rocks.

And riding into the hills on their bikes with ropes

and nets in the hope of catching a white crow and winning the thousand-pound reward announced by the company that made White Crow tomato sauce ("ketchup" had more years to catch on). No white crow was spotted, let alone captured; not by anyone.

Every man including his father wore a hat, a custom which gradually died out. Boys, including him, went around with pocketknives. And it was common too for men to carry one in their trousers, sometimes on a fine chain, ready to peel an apple. Sunglasses came later, even though the harsh light had always been there. Perhaps encouraged by American films—James Dean, Gregory Peck, McQueen—it wasn't long before everyone seemed to be wearing sunglasses.

On the footpath outside a car-wrecking yard, next to Cruikshank's milk bar, a man sat for hours on end on a kitchen chair. In place of a missing arm he had a hook. It dominated his appearance. No-one thought to ask him what had happened. Sitting there in the sun he didn't seem at all upset or embarrassed about having lost an arm which had been replaced by a hook attached to a dark leather socket. Heavy-set, expressionless man. Have others remembered him seated on a chair on the footpath? Are there others who remember Mr Cruikshank pouring the cream? Does anyone remember him at all? Does his image appear without warning, without any reason? Or his silent sister? If remembered is it only because of the grubby shirt and the bulge disfiguring his hand, and the man on the chair remembered only because of his arm?

Cars were seen as intricate machines, possessing a density in all parts of their design. The aesthetics of each one prompted approval or not, their specifications and performance were known in detail. And each car displayed the values of those who drove them. There were Sporting Car Clubs and gymkhanas. Young men who somehow owned MGs with wire wheels went about in corduroy trousers and desert boots. A few were seen wearing cravats. Threading their way through this light traffic were other men on motorbikes with sidecars, taking their wife and kids on a trip somewhere.

The cars drove across the rectilinear city, stopping,

moving forward, the long and the short, like a loom producing an oily cloth. The streets were so empty a sports car made an inordinate noise, attracting the admiration of young boys in groups who made imitations of the sound of gear-changing, or even by a man walking by himself along the street. 'But that passion for machines would pass as everything passes.' The cars were mostly small sedans with archetypal names from England, Morris Oxford, Wolseley, Austin, Humber (after the river), the Ford Prefect and Anglia. Graziers favoured the bigger cars, American. Those large low-revving engines and utilitarian simplicity, efficient, pragmatic, suited the long distances of Australia. Every car had a length of fencing wire in the boot, and it was surprising how often it was needed. On country roads a canvas water bag was slung over the front bumper bar. It was front-page news the day the new Holden was revealed. For the first weeks men would stop in the street when one drove past, and coming across one parked they stood around it nodding and looking thoughtful. If they were lucky the owner lifted the bonnet for them. People wanted one. Those who had the money to actually buy one put their names on a waiting list. It could take anything up to four or five months before they could drive one away and be the envy of neighbours. According to General Motors it was "Australia's Own Car", an early example of untruth or an incomplete fact which people nevertheless wanted to hear and accept. From then on a certain scepticism was born in him, not always healthy.

On the Sunday afternoon drives, seated between his two brothers and sister in the Vauxhall, his father bent over the steering wheel hardly saying a word, they waited for Noarlunga Hill to come into view, south of the city. In the summer a dozen or more English cars would have their bonnets up, boiling. Clearly these cars were not suited to Australian conditions, yet were still being shipped out. Even he, aged thirteen, could sense something was wrong. Only later did he see it as an early sign of the decline of the British Empire, well before fingers were pointing to Suez; in both cases, institutions within an institution found it too difficult to adjust.

Large gaps remained between objects and between people, and between earth and sky. Vast gaps in memories—almost entirely gaps—as there were in the unaccountable hours, days and years of his life. Agriculture entered the city. If there was a drought the grass of the parklands turned like litmus to white-yellow, the leaves dried and flew about, while large sprinklers made the helpless hissing sound of insects. Dunking a biscuit, so widespread it was rare for one going soggy to break off and float in the tea, to be fished out with a spoon. Crows from the inland settled in the city trees and could be heard from the GPO. And "crow's feet" spread from the eyes of tired women. A dry squinting face took hold, nationally.

Children were given the names Rex, Lance, Raylene, Cyril, Lynette, Bev.

In Mr Townsend's grocery on the corner there were breakfast cereals stacked to the ceiling, like rows of books; to retrieve one he used a broom handle which had a bottle top nailed at one end and caught the box in his arm as it tumbled down. With another boy he'd stand inside the shop waiting for this to happen. Attractive too was the sawdust on the floors of butcher shops—enough to ask what sort of person started the habit, also where did all the sawdust come from? Shandies were taken out to women waiting in the hotel car park, buckets were metal. If anyone wanted a bottle of olive oil they had to go to the chemist.

No swearing at home. 'Struth!' was forbidden, it being short for 'God's truth', and 'Gee!' was frowned upon, it was taken from 'Jesus'. At the same time his mother said, 'Don't sit on the concrete step, you'll get worms.' From his father, 'Procrastination is the thief of time.' If he was corrected at the table by a fact, he would nod, 'Mister Exacto.'

Which twin has the Toni?

Men took jobs in the public service—for security.

His mother had been a milliner. From a shelf in the wardrobe she took down a folder of watercolours and handed them to him one at a time. 'I did these.' They were of flowers with long stems and delicate leaves. She spoke as if sorry to have stopped painting, or seeing again a future she may have missed. She made up for it by having flowers on the curtains, on cushion covers and on the sofa, the shower screen and towels in the bathroom, the tea towels, and on the small cardboard box for holding buttons, sunflowers. She invariably had a flower pattern for her dresses, often turquoise—many small flowers. She also did the flowers for the church, filling the boot of the car, and when another woman did them by mistake she took them out of the vases and replaced them with her own. She had two sisters, two brothers. She saw more of Evelyn than the older sister. One brother, Reg, was a postman who delivered on foot in the city centre. In his forties he placed a matrimonial advertisement in a rural newspaper, and to everyone's surprise a river-woman with two small boys all with blond hair came forward, and he married her.

A conscientious objector during the war: he was made a stretcher bearer on the Kokoda Trail.

His mother having a cup of tea and cake in the lounge room with the woman in mauve, powdered face, smeared lipstick, gloves. 'She was the most beautiful one at school, and as we grew up,' his mother said after she left—strolling up the street to catch the tram—'she had many proposals, but no man was good enough, and so she is by herself.'

His mother's kindness to his father.

Photograph on the sideboard of his mother on her

honeymoon on Kangaroo Island, smiling through a hole in a rock.

Because he had had more than one wife his mother spoke to him freely about women, as if he had special knowledge of them.

Mr Huffadine opposite who didn't mind a barren front yard—his bushy eyebrows—was never seen in the garden, never mowed the lawn—gave them his copies of *Saturday Evening Post* which featured American cars in colour, often with their hoods lifted to display the broad two-tone seats, like one of Elvis Presley's shirts. Gradually Australia headed towards the *Saturday Evening Post* world of combed hair and perfectly clean teeth, the post-war picture of prosperity and optimism, which appeared simple, as shown in microscopic detail by the magazine's favourite, Norman Rockwell, who many saw as having more truth in his front covers than anything painted by Vermeer. The energy and the curse of popular culture... It was not unusual to hear someone singing their way to the bus stop: *Gee, it's great after being out late / Walking my baby back home...* The local cars became longer and larger, soon outstripping the imported British ones which remained altogether too cramped, lacking in ambition.

The Stewart sisters, Nancy and Jean. Out of curiosity and adventure one of them, Nancy, allowed him to try kissing her behind a hedge.

Their father had green eyes.

People played tennis or went to the Botanical Gardens and sat on a rug and ate curried-egg sandwiches while they watched the swans. Away from the city they gathered under a gum tree alongside a slow-moving brown river, the men submerging their bottles of beer in wheat bags to cool them down, although his father never drank a drop and his mother only took a sip of brandy for medicinal purposes. In the men's lavatories he accompanied his father and looked across with envy at the enormous size of the slack penises of grown-up men. It was hot. It was hardly possible to walk in bare feet. Even the lawn was hot. At a waterhole in the River Torrens spotting some dentures on a tree trunk, and a man yelling out from the water, 'Put 'em back!'

To be forced on hot mornings and afternoons to

attend church. The mournful, mournful hymns and singing. During prayers everybody closed their eyes, some very tightly; and he asked his mother why. As for sermons and religious instruction: their words moved about in the unknown, about what could not possibly be known. The almost insufferable tedium was enlivened only when a preacher attacked dancing or the wearing of lipstick. Philosophy—Schopenhauer, Hume to begin—became useful to him. With philosophy came an eagerness to live and learn.

While sawing some wood in the garage his father without looking in his direction warned him off seeing a girl from Gawler, because she was Catholic. When he moved to Melbourne she followed and stayed two weeks. In the morning she wore blue satin slippers decorated with white pompons, which displayed contentment and the necessity of a certain tartiness. Thirty years later she traced his number and phoned from a town in Queensland. During the conversation she said her husband and daughter had been killed some months earlier in a car crash.

Earliest memory (c. 1943): waking up in his cot in

the hot bedroom facing west, the honey-coloured light coming in through the holland blind. Enough to make him begin to cry.

Next door were the Wilsons—no children. Occasionally he spoke, the wife did not. They were the only ones in the street to employ a gardener, Mr Palmer, a large man who worked on his knees in a navy-blue singlet, without a shirt. He didn't mind a boy squatting alongside as he weeded or grunted over a spade. The morning he slipped headfirst into the fishpond, Mr Palmer yanked him out by the ankles. Wiping his face and clothes with his handkerchief, he said, 'Don't tell your mother.' Even then, aged ten, he understood certain things you do not tell a mother/woman.

On the way to school, the blacksmith's yellow dog said to be part-dingo and always sitting at the gate bit him as he reached out to pat it.

Chicken was a luxury served only on Christmas Day,

followed by tinned pineapple and junket. A fridge had replaced the icebox; a round green washing machine on wheels replaced the copper and wringer; an electric mixer stood at the ready on the bench. A fluorescent light gave a touch of modernity, or prosperity, enough for neighbours to come in and look up in wonder at the tube on the ceiling.

Adults never discussed politics. No-one said who they had voted for. 'Nobody should earn four times more than anybody else,' his father's one political statement.

Father's black-and-white photograph of Ingrid Bergman fixed with drawing pins to the inside of the 'medicine chest', so called, in the kitchen. The formidable effect of film, of *Casablanca*, and of the photographic image, the power of popular culture. Towards the end of his career Louis Armstrong came through Adelaide and played the trumpet with a gleaming white handkerchief in one hand, as did Johnnie Ray, who fell on his knees and wept on stage while singing. He went to both concerts and instead of being moved felt awkward, embarrassed for them going through the motions.

Time which doesn't vary offers a certain regularity,

while everything within it is uneven and jumbled.

To be intelligent and natural. Does one interfere with the other?

With his sister in the afternoon walking at the far end of Christie's Beach, school holidays. A slender woman in bathers screaming and pointing to the water. Two men ran past, one stopped and gave him his watch to hold. As he and his sister waited, a man was carried from the water and laid on the sand. Holding the lifesaver's watch he felt part of the rescue. The young woman on her knees on the sand, now with an old face, making strange wailing sounds, her husband a body face down.

The woman and the two men running to the rescue are now also dead. Only he is left to preserve the image of a particular tragedy which is about to disappear when he too is dead.

Pix and other magazines gave the vital statistics, such as 36–19–34, below photographs of a film star or a model or a young woman wanting to be a model, each happy to pose in two-piece bathing costumes. And he could not help glancing at the shapes of the women and checking the figures, as printed. Gradually this information was reduced until it was not offered at all.

Remember Billy Graham? He landed in Adelaide and filled the showground. But by then every man worked Brylcreem into their hair: *A little dab'll do you.*

Haircuts were done by his father who sat him under the trellis near the tank stand and yanked his head if he fidgeted even slightly. For a special occasion or to repair the efforts of his father he was occasionally sent to the barber on Magill Road, now gone. An exceptionally neat shop, two chairs, the one near the window worked by his wife. Both the barber and his wife were thin and unsmiling, each in a white coat. As they worked, the barber smoked a cigarette in a black holder and would sometimes talk across to his wife about things which had nothing to do with hair. Now that his hair has virtually stopped growing, unlike his fingernails, the amount of time spent having his hair cut can be looked upon with real affection. The leather chairs were black with large armrests, a set of chrome-plated levers and a swivel chair attached for the barber to rest while working, chairs so elaborate and practical his father said they could only have been made in the United States. And they did summarise the technical edge of America, the way they excelled at product. Above the mirror in a gold frame was a large painting of a mountain lake of unnatural blue-ness with pine trees nearby, snow on the mountains and a clear sky of such painstaking detail it quickly became uninteresting. It had attracted the barber and his exceptionally neat wife, but made him forever wary of paintings in the photorealist style.

Aware of his father's sudden temper, which was followed by a sadness around the eyes.

At night with his father and Ian Monfries, a photographer on crutches (polio victim), in the gravel drive waiting for the first Sputnik to pass over. 'There she blows!' he pointed with his crutch. A faint silvery path crossed the night sky among the stars. Satisfied he said, 'That was history. And we saw it.'

Girls were both soppy and obscure. Boys surveyed them with confused mockery.

Memories are unequal. Some don't need searching for; they appear randomly. Others need a concentrated effort to recall.

Going off to sleep as rain fell on the tin roof, sounding not like water but tonnes of nails or gravel being poured.

Moving through spaces, hot paddocks. Hum and clicking of insects.

How the sight of the drowned man was followed by the accident at school. Mr Trainer, a popular teacher, his thick greying hair, was batting in the nets in the lunch hour. Four or five boys stood around fielding. Struck hard by Mr Trainer the ball hit the boy's head, only a few yards from where he was standing, making a soft-hard smacking sound. He was the first to reach the figure lying on the ground. As he looked down a large lump appeared on the side of the boy's head. His legs and head gave a slight shudder and stopped. The teacher on his knees, his hand covering his eyes.

Bodies would be seen on the street in Bombay,

where death is not hidden, in car crashes, in hospitals, at funerals, the mortuary in Melbourne, on the footpath in Kings Cross, Sydney. But it is the first deaths—the drowned man face down on the sand, followed by the boy with dark curly hair felled by the cricket ball—he has remembered.

In the hotel dining room for his mother's birthday, demonstrating to the rest of his family how to eat spaghetti bolognaise with a fork. Instead of pleasure at showing the ease of it, he felt smug. And his father was unimpressed.

Uncle Doug who lived at Largs Bay and worked in the Customs department taught him to swim. A completely bald man, he was patient and didn't mind sand in the house which was not far from the beach.

Before getting married, his father worked for a year or more on a cattle/sheep station in the outback, north of Cooper's Creek. The remoteness suited him. His mother died when he was eight. A shy man, he had gone inward early. He took a camera into the country, and using photo corners stuck the small prints of stockmen, Aboriginals and landscapes ('A Rocky View', 'Blacks' Graves') in a dark brown album. In group photographs he wrote in ink below each man, 'Tom', 'Roger', 'Long Ted', and identified himself with '?', not writing his name, an act of self-effacement not unusual then. He began a dictionary of local Aboriginal words; but nothing was made of it. The rural experience ran through his side of the family, although he never went back to the station. He travelled and camped in other parts of the state. Reading the newspaper, he first turned to the weather map—rainfall, possibility of. Every year there were stories of travellers dying of thirst. Never leave the car. The difficult-to-imagine case in 1953 of the Page family of five who had arrived from England only a few months earlier and drove off in the middle of summer to visit a son working in the outback. Others ran out of petrol, or became lost, or bogged in sand, and then ran out of water. To his father who read them out with grim satisfaction, they were 'mugs'. Stay with the vehicle! In 1957 living in the city with a family he too followed the manhunt for the killer in the Sundown Station murders and saw it as a turning point in the casual protocol of the bush: you always gave a hand, always gave a stranger a lift. 'Things will not be the same again,' he told them over breakfast. In his father's glass-fronted bookcase were some Georgette Heyer novels with orange spines, *What Katy Did Next*, and *The Story of San Michele*. There was also *On the Origin of Species*. The rest were the poets of the bush, Banjo Paterson and C. J. Dennis, and Henry Lawson, who would later appear on the ten-dollar note, along with a few histories of the mysterious explorers, some who set out on expeditions into the interior and completely disappeared. It was a landscape culture. The painters continued working through their impressions of the landscape. These had to be more or less settled before a young nation could move on to painting pure and simple. Composers too "illustrated" aspects of landscapes, setting the mangroves, rivers, the unpredictable seasons and the cockatoos to music. It was left for *Mad Max* careering about in the desert to be the most memorable film. And the novels, short stories and poems were set well away from the cities, 'The Drover's Wife', proclaiming the values of the bush and mateship, which was taken up by historians, although mates and mateship were common elsewhere, notably in Russian literature.

The dryness of voice and surroundings produced yarn-like literature, the 'dreary, dun-coloured realism' which lasted for many years. With eyes turned to the interior the population could mostly avoid the rest of the world. At the same time—almost the definition of provincial-ism—if anyone looked up with too much admiration at the standards set by civilisations above the equator it was condemned as 'cultural cringe'.

On the Birdsville Track he soon became bogged in the sand, 1964, white dingo near silvery Lake Frome, into the Flinders Ranges, and along rivers, eyes watering from the smoke of the campfire. At home it was he who was asked to kill a chicken, and did so with an axe, only dimly aware of what he was doing. He wanted to get away from the familiar streets, the ordinariness. He enjoyed the night skies and the coldness of dawn and then to creep behind bushes and shoot rabbits, kangaroos and ducks. He stepped around snakes. Hemingway, the Nick Adams stories, was certainly an encouragement. Then and later he imagined he could explain himself, see himself more clearly, through physical discomfort. 'Have you ever done anything dangerous?' As if by setting out to experience mild hardships as in Afghanistan, West Africa, and on the ships, etc. would give him wisdom and clarity denied to others.

His mother hurried out and gave a glass of water to the postman resting on his bike on a hot day.

Seeing a policeman in the middle of King William Street directing traffic: 'He's handsome.'

Almost every man was a smoker, many rolling their own, some could do it one-handed, unconcerned about having nicotine-stained fingers; in India large numbers of men and women had their teeth and lips stained blood-red with betel juice. For some it was the chance to develop a style, holding out a Zippo lighter, flicking the lid open and shut with a sharp click. Somehow smoking cigarettes passed him by, though accustomed to the smoke he enjoyed watching the ritual of others.

The damp armpits of teenage girls at the dance and although the same age how they regarded the ritual far more seriously.

Of the hundreds of facts—the many hundreds—taught

to him at school, almost all disappeared or settled as a bedrock of information called "general knowledge", to emerge now and then many years later, allowing him further to understand a subject or a means of comparison. What came forward more readily and without warning was the appearance and behaviour of a few teachers. The science teacher explained how the piston of a car engine has to stop when it reaches the top and then at the bottom of each stroke—stopping each time, even when high-revving. He said the greatest discovery yet to be made by man was perpetual motion. 'If you saw a finger on a footpath, how would you know which hand it came from—the left or right?' Still puzzling over the point of this question. Mr 'Lenny' Blaskett, pink all over and bald, which drew attention to his teeth—his hard-working, prominent teeth. As he tried his best to introduce classical music, it was not possible to avoid his teeth. With his gramophone from home placed on the desk he put on a Beethoven symphony and closed his eyes, his teeth came forward. On Sundays he played the organ at his church. Sitting at the school piano, which was between the desk and the door, he adopted an anxious, hurried manner more suitable to working the stops and keyboard of an organ. He enlisted the boy who could read music to sit beside him, as if it were an honour, and the class waited for the tentative page-turner to lose his way, which he soon did, and the music to be snatched away from him. The most unpopular teacher—he took it upon himself to explain the importance of hygiene in and around the genitals, erasing diagrams of foreskins on the blackboard as quickly as he drew one. He used the cane, a length of dowelling, which could draw blood, and for this he took the victim down to the lavatories, away from the eyes of the class. There he became almost friendly, making light of it, before raising his arm and eyes bulging, suddenly bringing the cane down on the hand, and repeating, depending on the offence. He told no-one in the school that he and Mr Blaskett were distantly related, on his mother's side.

Mr Kenny, his thick straight hair, and horn-rims. As he talked he smiled, or almost smiled. It was his way of imparting knowledge. When for no reason someone let out a laugh he came down between the desks and without a pause slapped him across the face. The boy looked up; saw Mr Kenny rattled by what he had done. He was perhaps the best teacher. On any given day at least one boy would have a broken arm in plaster, and be the envy of others. Bits of yellow sawdust on the hair and shoulders of the woodwork teacher. He was never seen out of his grey work coat. He was a teacher, yet hardly ever opened his mouth. He pointed and nodded, or else slowly shook his head. A likeable, mostly silent figure. On the wall behind him was a long strip of varnished wood, inlaid with the different timbers of Australia. Next door, the metalwork teacher: he had the thin silver moustache. His unpleasant way of washing his hands, which he did four or five times a day, a soft soapy motion, twisting his fingers. His crisply ironed short-sleeve shirt; never a tie. When something had been dropped in a lavatory bowl he marched everyone in and ordered a boy, one who had the most pimples, possibly the poorest, to put his hand into the water and fish it out. For lunch the metalwork teacher sat at his desk and cracked open a boiled egg, with cheddar cheese and a tomato. He used a pocketknife to peel an apple. Short and unusually thin art teacher who wore beige waistcoats. His way of teaching was to remain seated behind his desk at an angle to the class, his cheek on his hand. He had a slow, exhausted delivery. It was as if he were talking to another audience. His hair fell across his forehead. Someone began calling him 'Adolf'. On the hot afternoon, unable to control the class, he appeared to be ignoring the noise—until he jumped up and stood above someone sitting in the front, 'You, by Christ, I'll knock your block off!' Sitting down just as suddenly he put his face in his hands: 'I can't stand this any longer.' Once he brought in another teacher, Mr Lewis, who was an artist. Quite stout, a solid manner, dark moustache. He wore a tweed jacket buttoned up. If he was an artist, he looked like anybody else. He said that in a painting of a white sheet hanging on a clothes line, there might be half a dozen different colours, possibly even more.

Reading aloud in class *The Shadow-Line*; and when someone else was doing it, getting ahead of them. Small book with red cover. And *The Odyssey* (in prose). Was it at the other school?

Seeing on the page the 'versts' and 'sturgeons' of Russian literature.

Miss Murphy, who had red hair, felt the cold. She liked to have a fire in the classroom. Her method was to arrange the kindling horizontally into a geometric tower, while all the time talking over her shoulder, 'teaching', which had their father almost rolling on the floor laughing, to make a fire you need only a few twigs. Early evening as they were about to enter a cake shop in a different suburb, Miss Murphy was seen at a corner table with Mr Roberts, the headmaster. A large neat man, he usually wore a three-piece suit. Miss Murphy had put her hair up, the way she made a fire, and was leaning forward with her chin resting on her clasped hands. She was hardly recognisable. Their mother pulled them away before they were seen. 'He's married,' she almost hissed, 'and has two small children.'

Teacher who was short and thin, name long forgotten, who wrote a play to be performed on the tray of a truck on speech night. It was about a teacher in a classroom and the teacher himself played the teacher—and he too directed the play. Each boy was given an easy part. All he had to do was raise his hand, 'If a white hen lays a white egg, why doesn't a black hen lay a black egg?' Glancing down at the proud parents, including his mother, he thought they were laughing at him for believing such a ridiculous question. Each of the desks fitted with an inkwell in one corner.

He liked to think it was all happening around him, and he was to one side. The momentum on any popular subject was produced by others.

The school on Glen Osmond Road was barely two years old. With its modern cream-brick look it was assumed to be a good school. The main building of two or three storeys was set back, parallel to the road. In front was the oval; in summer the steady metallic hiss of its sprinklers. Behind the main building a creek ran through the grounds. Occasionally a boy slipped in, or was pushed. It sometimes flooded and we lined the bank, throwing things into the torrent, or just stood watching it, joined by some of the teachers. It felt odd to see nature rushing past, while lessons consisting of facts and possible figures were being taught in rooms.

Being given lessons by elders.

Teachers in the lunch hour strolling in pairs, smoking pipes.

In the tram on the way to work in the morning almost everyone reading a book, his shadow folding forward.

Sitting around the wireless in their dressing gowns,

concentrating on the difficult-to-follow, rapid, ping-pong commentary of the Davis Cup, Lew Hoad and Rosewall—something we were good at; or else 'Randy Stone' (private eye, American), and the quiz shows run by Jack Davey, 'Hi ho, everybody!' as he came on air, or his American rival, Bob 'Pick-a-Box' Dyer and his wife called Dolly, while their mother did the ironing. Later, *The Goon Show* on Friday night had them grinning at its silly voices which they imitated at tram stops, in offices, and at meal tables.

At school he joined the air cadets and on Thursdays wore the summer or winter uniform, learning drill, presenting arms, attending lectures, recognising the silhouettes of enemy aircraft, such as Heinkels and Messerschmitts, even though they had stopped flying long ago. The Flying Officer from the Second World War with a hoarse voice, 'All right, you're in the Cadet Corps. Say it out loud—"corps". Tack on an "e" and you'll get closer to war.' He went for two-week camps at Mallala Air Force Base where he did mess duty and fired Bren guns. But he suffered homesickness. He disliked the heavy boots, as issued, somehow managing to wear civilian black shoes, which can be seen in the group photograph of the cadets, all eighteen of them, in summer uniforms, seated, eager for battle.

The electric colours and magnesium-white patterns on November 5 curving upwards and coming towards, small unpredictable explosions of Jumping Jacks, the screams of women and girls, acrid smoke and darkness. (Too English to last, Guy Fawkes or "cracker night" was gradually replaced by the more professional fireworks of Chinese New Year.) In the morning skyrockets on their long sticks could be found where they had returned to earth. Going around collecting them—for no apparent reason—he was caught on a front lawn by a woman in a dressing gown. She was not at all punishing but gentle, and took an interest in him and his task, joining in the search. 'Let's see if there are any over there.' Probably no more than twenty, she had a film star's full cheeks. She married a famous Australian Rules footballer.

He began to notice the apparent gentleness of women, their patience, how their words had a psychological interest, their attentiveness, softer in attitude and manner than the bluntness of men. They were layered.

They were different.

His mother was softer than his father.

And she had done watercolours.

The first hand searching inside a bra: the rounded softness surprising him. Lying against a woman in bed, always the unexpected smoothness of her nakedness, except between their legs which suddenly added further to the mystery. Those that were soft, very soft, others wiry.

For a long time an albatross followed the ship, behind and above; apparently not uncommon.

Once having seen them—man with hook for arm—brother or sister pouring cream from a tin—faces of women on pillows washed with a contented smoothness—drowned man face down on Christie's Beach—sand dunes to the horizon—storms at sea—they are part of his life, only to disappear when he dies.

Before houses could be built a quarry had been allowed at the foot of the Adelaide Hills, which expanded until its yellow-white wound was visible from all parts of the city. A professional photographer explained that it reflected light, which came in handy when setting apertures, said as he bent over his elaborate plate camera, a Linhof.

I began writing out of dissatisfaction.

After weeks of cloudlessness, Bombay, the way it darkened late afternoon, the sky filled low with clouds, the stillness suddenly split open by the thunder, which finally loosened the humidity, followed by days of heavy rain (the 'monsoonal downpour') which darkened still further the streets, buildings and huddled figures, although lit up with sheet-lightning. The steps that turned into waterfalls, streets into rivers. The pale brown water had all sorts of urban rubbish and large leaves floating at the fringes. People tried wading. They wanted to get home. A different part of the earth where seasons too were noticeably different. He lived there for two years from 1968.

There were many more ordinary days in Bombay. Aside from the sweetish thickness of the heat it is the breaking of the monsoon, the expectation of it, the cracking thunder which finally split open the darkness of the day that remains.

In India he would come across western women, often American, some Australian, wearing saris. Somehow they were made to look broad-shouldered and flat-footed; and when they walked they did not glide as Indian women in saris did.

And his marriage in Melbourne (the old church in Kew), the coarseness of his speech ('she's getting her torso ready'), how marriage nevertheless steadied him, he felt it, and the pleasure of observing her contentment. He was welcomed into her family, and he hardly knew why. Her two younger sisters looked on with happy curiosity. Even then he was conscious of his instability which would only become worse, losing him marriages, friends and jobs. It was as if he needed to break loyalties by inviting others (and organisations) to reject him. They rented an apartment, later the furnished rooms of a house in Hawthorn owned by a woman much older. At night she could be heard falling over from the sherry, but they hardly noticed. Happiness gave them tolerance. On their honeymoon in a Sydney hotel he switched on the TV to the news that the prime minister, Harold Holt, had disappeared in the surf at Portsea.

Every day is different from the one before, and the one following. Only what he is remains the same—is at least more constant. He feels more constant within than he actually is.

The face of Mr Pinder, the dentist, came close enough for him see the pores on his nose and hear the sucking of the Pep-O-Mint Life Saver which he took to cut down the bad breath. He was never without a mint in his mouth. As he moved it around on his tongue he smacked his lips loudly, without realising; it had become habit. When one was finished he paused, even if in the middle of drilling, to unwrap another mint Life Saver from the roll in his trousers, and popped it in his mouth. Mr Pinder, who drove a large British saloon, had been to the same school as his father in Adelaide. It was assumed the family enjoyed a special discount for his dental work, although—for all his neatness, he had rough hands—Mr Pinder should have charged more for the difficult children he endured. It is the Pep-O-Mint on his breath and the neat silver moustache which have remained.

Apparently no memory is exact. And when written down the imperfection expands.

Prancing. A sort of Amadeus prancing-about in speech and manner, as if he didn't want to be taken seriously or appear stale and ordinary. Or, more likely, to obscure an approaching closeness—establishing a brief distance. It could only leave him looking uneven, not to be taken seriously.

New addresses. Melbourne, marriage. Bombay; London—three addresses; Sydney—the terrace house bought in Birchgrove; Melbourne (second marriage); Sydney—the three different apartments.

On the canal in northern France a small girl on a barge was going higher and higher on a swing set up by her father, a carefree, semi-circular movement in contrast to the horizontal forward movement of the barge. Why this insignificant image has remained was beyond him. On the footpath outside the bar in view of the container docks, Rotterdam, he looked on as three men in orange boilersuits fought with broken bottles, a matter of standing back and estimating their chances until the police arrived.

People began to say 'Kafkaesque' and 'surreal'. Very disappointing. Journalists described situations of the slightest complexity as 'existential threat', while architects were talking about a building's 'DNA'. These terms were parked in the background, ready to rush forward at the slightest opportunity.

Muddy ice in the park in Moscow which gave the impression of a river flooding through the wintry trees.

This earnest man moving about, seeking as many experiences as possible—thinking he was "experienced".

At his mother's funeral the men in their cheap, ill-fitting suits—only now having been away can he see they were cheap, ill-fitting—and their worn faces. Poor people. 'If looks could kill!'

Explosion down the coalmine north-east of Bangalore which almost threw him off his feet. Afterwards in his room above he read Emerson, and cannot remember which essay.

Bread and dripping after school—something else that would not happen today.

What began slowly has accelerated.

Frangipani flowers scattered on the lawn here.

Very little happened in his part of the world. There were no momentous events, none that already had the look of importance. They happened more in the higher latitudes, the United States, Europe, so far away they required only passing interest. Later, the moments of assassinations—Martin Luther King, the two Kennedys, Sadat—and images of war—Vietnam, most of all—and extreme weather and mass happiness and other strong images filled the pages of *Life* magazine. What was presented in black-and-white at arm's length remained as a residue, faintly remembered; histrionics at the UN, a shoe-banging on the lectern; Cuban missile crisis, the stretching of anxiety; referendum vote in Australia to embrace Aboriginals; Hungary—the tanks; Berlin Wall dismantled; Suez, 1956; a man actually walking on the moon—incredible; Jean Shrimpton in miniskirt at Melbourne Cup; Ike playing golf—another bald head; Woodstock; various nuclear tests; Israel at war, again; great rivers in flood—later down to a trickle; the famines; death of Stalin, Churchill, Macmillan, R. G. Menzies, de Gaulle, Nehru, Ernest Hemingway, Christina Stead, and many more—and some he actually knew; small wars in small countries; the marriages of film stars; four-minute mile; regularity of elections—surprising how each one contained such interest; they never found Harold Holt's body. Fires. The usual volcanoes. Earthquake damage. The larger size of battleships, the aircraft carriers; Comet airliner—its beauty before it crashed; later, the Concorde; the fall of Saigon—those figures hanging on to American helicopters; British PMs and MPs in their pinstripes looking hopelessly out of time and place; royals and their weddings; Patrick White won the Nobel Prize—he died; the entire animal world was beginning to look helpless;

those twin towers coming down, as in some disaster movie—and the consequences; vaccine for polio; many thousands of refugees crossing deserts or overloading boats; the spread of radical Islam too widespread for any comfort; that solitary coatless man standing in front of tank, Tiananmen Square, briefcase of a clerk in one hand, his modest bravery. Here images reeled off join others momentarily forgotten. All from a distance, via static or slowly moving photography, not experienced at all. Although silent it has been described as 'noise'.

In Bombay the newspapers were printed on coarse newsprint with hardly any photographs. Keeping up with the rest of the world was through *Time* and *Newsweek*. And there were other ways of having opinions changed. Opening the screening of *The Battle of Algiers* at the 1968 Bombay Film Festival the Mexican ambassador, Octavio Paz, began slowly, then built up to a vitriolic denunciation of the Americans in Vietnam. The audience stood and applauded. Within a week the ambassador was recalled, and never returned. Between wars young men grow their hair longer. In the 1970s they grew long beards, and wore embroidered Afghani waistcoats, brown beads, Indian sandals. Young women with them wore long cotton skirts, and blouses which allowed their loose breasts to move and be seen to move. They sat on the ground peacefully. Others wrote messages on walls or took to the streets and hurled themselves at the lines of police; this was done with more ferocity across the United States and Europe.

Without obvious history was like walking without a shadow, or swimming without sight of land.

We have tried working our way into history by begging to be included in foreign wars.

'Give me a break!'

'Did you hear the one about — ?'

Parents standing together in the garage as he reversed out, small suitcase filled with clothes and a few books on the seat beside him. In the headlights they looked forlorn, but it was easy leaving Adelaide for what he believed to be a city and so a life of greater complexity, Melbourne. A few years earlier on a school trip to Melbourne, near the Botanic Gardens he looked up above the trees at the heavy fluttering of wings: his first helicopter. Lights of trucks seen from a long distance. The bird that hit the windscreen. In the boarding house in South Yarra seven men slept in the one room—complexity and ordinariness combined. Most were carpenters and concreters working on the freeway being built along the Yarra River. If he began reading in bed one would step over without a word and turn out the light. As he had already sensed with men, he had to be careful in what he said. It took very little for an unhappy man to come forward resorting to arms and fists as a language. At nineteen everything still seemed new. In the office in South Melbourne the wilder you were after hours the more friends you had. Women not yet twenty were happily on the pill and every young man gave a display of extreme drinking. The women liked Barossa Pearl. Otherwise it was schooners at the saloon bar, or bottles of beer at someone's place, wine yet to make the inroads. Instant coffee arrived. Everyone had a Nescafé tin in the kitchen. Only a few cafes served an espresso in the tiny cups, but as more migrants arrived from Europe this naturally increased, beginning in Melbourne, and in certain suburbs small tables began to creep out onto the pavement, a movement which spread, eventually into country towns. Sales of tea and teapots went into corresponding decline. Black bread could be bought, although it looked more brown than black.

As the post-war prosperity continued new restaurants appeared, taking over ordinary shopfronts or hotel dining rooms, many closing after only a few months.

For a long time the streets of Melbourne remained new to him. He'd come across buildings and street corners never seen before. It made him imagine other cities he hadn't seen, Vienna, as in *The Third Man*, Paris, and Calcutta in black-and-white from Satyajit Ray films, and Istanbul, perhaps Alexandria. In the shop behind the office the large woman working with her husband buttering bread for sandwiches had a number tattooed on her muscular forearm. In Adelaide, the Weiss family lived in the next street. Every evening they would leave their neat white house and stroll around the block always in the same direction, the quietness of Adelaide encouraged Mrs Weiss to take her husband's arm, a small man. As they passed, each one nodded politely but never stopped. Their son Peter, who wore rimless glasses, became a successful surgeon. Only years later did they realise Weiss was not spelt nor pronounced 'Wise'. Mr and Mrs Weiss and their son have all died, although their son Peter Weiss, the surgeon, continues in the lives he has saved.

At the table he removed the bones of the fish for her

and enjoyed the feeling of gentleness.

He still thinks it possible that as explained by the geography teacher the word 'news' came from North–East–West–South. Already he had worked out that 'nap' was from Napoleon who had the ability to nod off for five minutes in the saddle and wake up completely refreshed. At least that was his thinking.

Somehow darker than dove-grey the streets of Melbourne which blended into the skies became intricately linked to the happiness of his first marriage, its innocent pleasures, including the close proximity of his wife's family, which seemed to replace his own family who lived far away in Adelaide. With cheery informality his in-laws would drop by in the evening, and their daughter would happily add to the meal, sometimes playing cards afterwards, all of which he enjoyed, and yet he found conversing with them difficult, often not knowing what to say. They were beer drinkers and smokers: one smoked and the other would reach out and take a puff. This too was a display of intimacy unusual to him. He looked on with envy at the ease of his young wife's devotion to them. It had a naturalness which was missing between the members of his own family.

By then writing—in his spare time—but not writing as he came to know it, more a forcing of regularity to establish the habit of writing something every day. And this determination almost made him believe he was a writer. Certainly he was behaving differently to everybody else; he didn't know anyone else who sat at a table writing every morning and weekend. It increased his curiosity. If it was not a story, he was writing observations of what was nearby. And so his stories appeared in the small literary magazines, there were at least half a dozen publishing fiction. But he became a "writer" only after he had a book published in 1975, followed by others, by which time he almost disliked the idea of being a "writer". Showing wonderful tolerance, his wife was attentive to his efforts, strict and tedious though they must have been for her.

The morning the telephone rang in the office and he picked it up automatically, to be told by the level voice of his brother speaking from Adelaide that their father with little warning had died from a heart attack during the night. He was fifty-two. The shock he felt hasn't been exceeded since. The greatest shocks have been in reaction to sudden, unexpected loss. On this morning he went into the washroom, in case someone stepped into his office, and stood looking at his face in the mirror. He felt entirely different from a few minutes before, and he studied the face before him for any change, whether his sorrow showed.

Somewhere in West Africa he saw a boy leading a blind man whose hand on his shoulder had worn a hole in his khaki shirt.

At least once a week there was a cloud formation ready to be admired.

A gradual, then rapid increase in prosperity.

Women including his wife took to wearing the "muu-muu" dress. It was gown-like, reaching almost to the ankles. Usually in bold colours, some had large flower patterns. The women wearing them clustered together at outdoor parties, or a woman would greet her dinner guests wearing one. Virtually nothing of their body shape could be seen. And yet the muu-muu dresses represented unreserved gaiety. It didn't last long. Attention soon turned to another fashion, while the gaiety, the innocent contentment of the women in Melbourne, remained.

After experimenting with the Windsor knot, men had decided in the new century not to wear a necktie. Cabinet ministers, company directors and waiters in fancy restaurants faced the public in pale blue or white shirts undone at the neck. It gave them a fresh, energetic look. And to think that his father had worn a woollen tie when gardening or mixing some concrete for a path around the house. The idea of jeans was imported from America, very practical and considered cool with the T-shirt. It was followed by "sneakers". These were once known as "sandshoes", to be worn playing tennis or walking on coral. (Of course, of course.) Along with the open-neck shirt "sneakers" began to be worn on all occasions by men, and women too, even high-fashion models. It was not unusual to see a man in a smart suit wearing "Nikes". They gave to the wearer an aura of mobility. Within a few decades Nike had become a recognisable brand, within touch of Coca-Cola and Google. At the same time the taste of tomatoes and broad beans gradually turned bland, as if being mass-produced indoors.

Hondas had replaced the heavy British motorcycles. Helmets were not compulsory. Cars had developed a sameness in appearance: it was really difficult to recognise the different makes. Except in the rarest of cases, cars hadn't been fitted with seatbelts. There seemed to be more and more car parks. Bowling alleys and drive-in picture theatres became popular. To meet the demand for drive-ins, properties were acquired and demolished. Young couples sliding about on the bench seats of their fogged-up cars were not at all interested in the film on the big outdoor screen. Drive-ins offered a site for intimacy which was public while at the same time private. There was otherwise nowhere else for couples to go to practise the rites of courtship. Only when it became possible to share apartments and thousands had moved in together did the drive-in theatres go into decline, leaving behind large areas of desolate asphalt.

The night on King William Street at about six o'clock when a body landed with a thud in front of him and lay face down. He squatted beside him. A line of dark blood flowed from his head. To the crowd that gathered he explained the man in an old coat had fallen from the roof, a suicide. The police arrived. 'It's Les again.' Turning him over one said, 'Broken nose.' He hadn't fallen from the roof after all. Drunk, he had fallen forward from a doorway. Again it is the extreme event, not an ordinary happy one, that reappears as an image.

The levelling between genders, the differences between men and women were being reduced at every opportunity. Was it in any way due to liberal democracy which had evened out aesthetics, and opinions, and differences between men and women—one opinion has equal weight to another? In Melbourne he had read Simone de Beauvoir, in Bombay in 1970 *The Female Eunuch* and *The Golden Notebook*, which seemed, as he listened and looked out on the street, out of sync. The indignant energy of these and other writers pushed him into thinking about the position of women, though he could not say whether his behaviour changed. He couldn't help being drawn to women, who were intricate and there close by. After which an imbalance remained.

Two people living together—marriage—is a daily experiment.

Artists, critics and anyone else in Melbourne interested in paintings were given a jolt in 1967 by 'Two Decades of American Painting', organised by MoMA. For a long time it was all they could talk about. These American painters went for scale without apparent limits, displaying a slashing sort of confidence like a team of many different Picassos—except that their paintings were mostly abstract, paintings that consisted only of painting. Their exuberance left the local treatments of landscape and myths looking cramped and "historical", lacking in spontaneity. The Jasper Johns map went far beyond ordinary landscape. Along with friends he went to the exhibition three or four times. He can still "see" the Gorkys and Rothkos, the Joan Mitchells, Reinhardts, Barnett Newmans. There was one solitary Jackson Pollock. Included were pop artists inflating the idea that anything could be the subject for painting, even comic strips. He still has the catalogue with the de Kooning woman on the cover. The exhibition overwhelmed many local painters who set about producing versions of the new American painting. While the Americans in one way or another reflected their own place, the Australian painters of colour field, or hard-edge, or even of pop, looked to be without a country. It was the painters who stayed with the interpretation of the local landscape who survived, cramped though some of their results were.

How an experience of art can leave valuable traces.

Years later many of the American paintings began to appear to him over-confident—often confidence was their subject—and over-scaled. A Chinese or Japanese calligrapher would have shaken their heads at the enormous sizes required by Franz Kline and Gottlieb, Newman and others for their work to produce an effect. At an artist's studio in Sydney he met Clement Greenberg who told him that major art only comes from the centre. For example, Francis Bacon was a minor artist.

He was happy in Melbourne, happy in marriage. As he grew accustomed to Melbourne or parts of it and became accustomed to marriage he felt the spread of restlessness which he did little to resist. Size alone made Melbourne more interesting than Adelaide, and with it always came the hint or the promise of greater interest. But the limits were known. Robert Louis S. had already looked at a map and said, 'When I think of Melbourne, I vomit…' And many talented young people had left for Europe, and even Canada, never to return. Closer to the problem was de Chirico in his curious novel, *Hebdomeros*. The first few sentences offer a view of Melbourne, its 'air of tedium and melancholy, a certain desolation, that particular atmosphere which pervades Anglo-Saxon towns on Sundays'. It hardly matters that de Chirico had never set foot in Melbourne, and that his description could apply equally to his deserted piazzas and the flags, statues and distant steam trains he positioned to throw melancholy shadows. Luckily he came across *Hebdomeros* in London long after he had left Melbourne. By then he understood the restlessness of Stendhal. He was also impressed with Stendhal's use of various *noms de plume*—to want to be anonymous, that is brave.

The curse of Methodism. No use denying it.

So much continues to be in reaction to it, either by lapsing into simple thought or working too hard forcing a thought not to be simple.

'Have a nice day', first heard in Amsterdam, 1970,

from an American sitting on a step outside the Stedelijk Museum. An attractive phrase, but no more.

The sand ankle deep inside the mosque.

Being a pallbearer at his father's funeral he looked across at his brother carrying the other side, and saw he was staring straight ahead. The two pallbearers bringing up the rear were from the funeral parlour. One had a handlebar moustache. Otherwise he cannot remember where it took place, or any of the surroundings, or what the weather was like. Their mother was unable to attend. She was in bed in the spare room, blinds drawn, not in the bedroom she had shared with him and where he had died. The younger brother was in Vietnam. He would have been called in by the army chaplain and told.

Food was served after the funeral to continue the living.

It had been experienced by many before him: returning home from living in another city to find the street and the family house had a plain, shrunken appearance. All the houses in the street looked smaller. No movement came from them. His house seemed to have moved a few feet closer to the street. Inside, the rooms were smaller than he remembered and he noticed how the floorboards creaked. A certain emptiness within him added to these impressions. And returning to Melbourne, which was still not familiar, it was he who felt diminished.

The distance between the living and the nearby dead—

The small contentments of married life. They began to buy paintings. One of his wife's friends left for overseas because everybody did it—for adventure. Most headed for England, then to Italy and Greece. She went to Toronto, married a doctor and had children, where she remained after they divorced. The other women friends in Melbourne were from the office, good-natured, happy drinkers in disappointing situations with careless young men.

From his mother he was taught how to hold a spoon and not eat noisily. A certain way of living plainly, frugally, was taught by example, by his father. As soon as he found a job his father recommended he join a Suit Club, as he had. Weekly payments were made, and after a few years there was enough to pay for a suit.

And now he knew words will continue when he too is dead, and without his words. It was something he could never talk about, not even to his wife who would have listened carefully while giving the appearance of not listening.

The lives of the philosophers had become almost as worth considering as their philosophies. For some reason not many had married. And it would be hard to imagine Schopenhauer, Nietzsche, Kant, Wittgenstein, Spinoza, Kierkegaard, or even David Hume involved in the intricacies of married life. There were others too. Socrates and Heidegger would appear to be exceptions that prove the rule. He looked about him for people to talk to about this, such was his lack of definition.

He wanted to 'think thoughts'. He wanted to see the world independent of those nearby. To remain independent he ignored the ideals of political parties, even political discussions of most kinds, since they were voices of the majority. Political activities registered as photographic images or distant voices. He looked for experiences away from what was common, if not actual experiences then from reading. He believed he was doing this naturally. That was his line of thinking.

In Ballarat Gardens the untidy man behind the palm tree who stepped out waving his penis at him, a small boy, as he passed. There was the shadow from rocks across the white road in Provence. The unexpected muddy-brown of the Arabian Sea was disappointing. In front of him inside the mausoleum the small Russian woman in headscarf fainted at the sight of Lenin laid out horizontal in his blue-black suit. The flock of pigeons in Adelaide in precise formation keep on repeating their switch of direction. Certain faces keep coming forward, some of unknown people (the woman with pegs in her mouth managing to smile while putting clothes on the line). Man in shirt sleeves choking on a fishbone in the restaurant, South Melbourne. She who lived with her sister on the rural edge of Melbourne, her galumphing ageing figure, much older than him, who disliked the size of her nose 'because of the shadow it made'. As he brushed her hair in the hospital the day before she died, she smiled slightly without opening her eyes, a rare experience of intimacy. How single, brooding women often become psychologically acute. He keeps seeing others who have died. Their increasing number give him the illusion he'll soon be one of the few left. The majestic rise of her hips—woman's hips. The varied cries of women during lovemaking. The different memories held by his parents were erased when they died, as these images will be.

Images which keep appearing without reason encourage seemingly unrelated lesser images. Most common are moments of beauty, such as the sheer elegance of nature—of a small part of the world—or else extreme experiences, usually violent. On the way to Brisbane as he passed the Volkswagen it moved over too suddenly and into the dirt and rolled over. He stopped and reached the car on its side to help the two women, one screaming.

A steady optimism was felt in all directions. Melbourne's architecture of solid stone demonstrated regularity on a daily basis, the futility of change. Discussions were cheery. He was conscious of being contented. He accepted it, yet was not satisfied. It was not enough. He could not feel his experience growing. They were a happy young couple and in such good health it was never questioned. The parents-in-law were invited for meals so they could see everything was working out well. He remembers in detail more of growing up in Adelaide than the six or so years as an adult in Melbourne. On an otherwise ordinary weekend they crossed town to a film festival in St Kilda to see Satyajit Ray's 'The Apu Trilogy'. Literature to him had always been superior to film, deeper, more spacious, etc.; yet in the darkened theatre, as he sat absorbed in the simple story told in black-and-white of the stages in Apu's life, as a child, a youth, a young newly married (by accident) man, it really was a matter of entering another world and being greatly altered by it. In *Aparajito*, the second film, Apu is shown living in a room above a busy railway station. As a way of living it looked both basic and layered. The room was small and bare with grubby walls. It was without the comforts he had become accustomed to in Melbourne; yet Apu was happy to be living and didn't notice. Looking down at the various train tracks with Apu he saw the future as an expanse of various possibilities, close to the movements of others. It would be a life somewhere back to the essentials. Apu was smiling at the prospect; while he, seated with his wife in the theatre in Melbourne on a Sunday afternoon, saw it was the way to acquire experience and precision, and possibly wisdom—wisdom through difficulty. It was soon decided. Together they would go to India, not just as visitors but living and working there. He said to himself he would even like to live in the same bare grubby room above a Calcutta railway station.

As a boy of about twelve when his father drove him in the night to Mannum on the River Murray to see for themselves the lines of men under floodlights hurriedly filling and passing sandbags as the flood dribbled and elsewhere poured over the edge.

Along St Kilda Road in the tram the man standing beside him who had bad teeth. He also had short fingernails. Of the many hundreds of people he had stood alongside in the Melbourne trams only this man has been remembered, all because of his teeth and matching fingernails.

When he thought of some other distant place he also thought of where he was standing.

If someone was disliked they were called 'shit-for-brains'.

Words he hadn't seen before he dutifully wrote down in a notebook, such as the one describing the apparent arch of the sky. The list grew into many pages, unusual-looking words which had resisted regular use and would never become smooth and ordinary as coins or stones. Meanwhile, writing them down gave the pleasant illusion he had accumulated something more.

The city called Bombay, mid-1968, was barely visible, a few lights twinkling below, the rest darkness. And driving in from the airport on either side was darkness with a few figures crouching over cooking fires or walking alongside the road, as if it was in a scattered village, not one of India's largest, most modern cities. Here and there orange lights suggested the direction of the road. It was made darker still by the habit or the law, back then, of cars not using their headlights, just the parking lights. Taxis were small, painted yellow and black, with shrill horns. Many drivers had a way of driving with one arm dangling out the window. A slow melancholy came in from the darkness and the few human forms, a display of poverty as a form of seepage. From the car entering the city the future was not visible, not even a suggestion of it. When he wound the window down the warm air came in with the smell of human shit, rotting vegetation and smoke. Closer to the city centre more people appeared on the street, in brown clusters, and stalls selling small items had electric lights. Buildings became taller and had a messy grey stain and shops or stalls jammed in along the ground floor, the pavements now crowded, but still the cars and taxis drove without headlights. There were palm trees. The shape of their serrated fronds fitted with the heat and melancholy. So strong and varied were the sights in the midst of congestion he looked from one thing to another and couldn't decide what to concentrate on. What was he doing there? he heard himself ask. How to adapt?

The brown building on Sir Phirozshah Mehta Road, fourth floor. The office and its ceiling fans. It was the far outpost of an American advertising firm, the manager an affable hands-on New Yorker, his loud and democratic laugh. The accountant was a tubby Scotsman, unmarried, dabbing with a handkerchief his watery blue eyes. In his short-sleeve shirt he looked even more like a merchant seaman as he waved happily when spotted surrounded by girls in a room behind the 'street of cages', as called, the red-light district of Bombay. His name is now forgotten. About thirty Indian staff worked in the department.

Men and women sat at desks or angled drawing boards, the men wearing nylon shirts, the women saris of yellow, blue-green and other colours, their cholis exposing a large expanse of bare back. The women and the men both had an open gaze, the women innocent in their direct questions.

It was 1968, the students at Tokyo University followed Paris. They had taken over the campus. A law student led him past the police lines and into the assembly hall; in expectation of a police charge a maze at the entrance had been constructed out of filing cabinets. Inside was a barricade of chairs and desks. He sat to one side as student leaders around a table discussed tactics. 'Capitalism', 'socialism', 'communism' were the only recognisable words amid the flow of incomprehensible Japanese. Only one Cézanne painting could be seen in Australia. In Tokyo at the head office of the Bridgestone Tyre Company the founder's collection of French art on permanent display included three paintings, two drawings of bathers. Standing before each of them, he began to see Cézanne's strange attraction. Cézanne was more personal, more modern than Manet, Renoir, Monet, and even Degas, hanging nearby. The painter's hand with all its hesitancies and adjustments was left exposed. To anyone who said Cézanne couldn't 'draw' he gave a pitying look. The outlines giving shape to trees or a mountain or a figure were left as art lines, a sign of the brush. With the gaps left on the canvas the viewer was forced to complete the picture. At least that is what he has felt ever since. Coming across the Cézannes on the way to Bombay was an early addition to his experience, the importance of which continues to this day, as he steps forward to contemplate another Cézanne.

How visual experiences vary, and are difficult to measure: at the Peace Memorial Museum in Hiroshima the long corridor of cubicles containing clocks, musical instruments, clothing, etc. at the instant of the explosion. A piano was porcupined with splinters, the hands of clocks and wristlet watches melted at the same moment of time. The force of the display was made still stronger by the slapdash arrangement of the identifying labels, some on bits of paper curling or slipping sideways on a pin, as if they had been assembled just a few minutes earlier. And the faulty translation in large letters over the exit which only increased the discomfort: instead of 'We Hope this Keeps the Peace', the first 'e' had been left off 'Peace'. Kenzō Tange who designed the horizontal museum was also the architect of St Mary's Cathedral in Tokyo. Here the soaring curves of concrete sent the eye upwards in praise of electric typewriters, transistors, and what wonders can be done with concrete—technical optimism. His first architectural experience: until then it had been limited to shearing sheds and bungalows with verandahs.

As we get to know a person there comes a point when we believe we know the person better than we know ourselves.

Thoughts of others he has written down:

Does awareness of another's faults constitute talent? —Stendhal

Leaves teach us how to die. —Thoreau

...Running wild with reason. —Maimon

The moderation of happy people... —La Rochefoucauld

Among people at any given moment in India the eye would be confronted by difficulty, man begging without arms, mother with naked child bloated with malnutrition. By tilting the head a fraction something else would be seen, beauty alongside ugliness, shy smile of child, woman's large eyes, grey cow with flowers on horns wandering among the crowd, length of brightly dyed cloth. His wife, who was gentle, became unhappy in the unfamiliar surroundings, away from her family. On her way to see him a group of country women surrounded her near Flora Fountain. Perhaps they hadn't been so close before to a European woman. One or two touched her with outstretched fingers. She was still agitated when he saw her. For a moment he wondered if this was part of "experience". At a cafe he told her that really there was nothing to be unhappy about, that in a strange country they should welcome the unexpected, they wouldn't be in India forever, they should preserve their curiosity wherever they were. She nodded, and he felt wise and successful—when a rat ran along the back of her chair and up the wall, and she leapt up and ran out onto the street.

On the first morning in Bombay they had been woken by sunlight coming through the curtains and the sound outside of metallic drumming. He opened the curtains. On the pavement a man watching the hotel kept his eye on the windows and fixed on him, and in a practised movement still drumming with one hand, placed a small boy on a seat on top of a pole and balanced it on his forehead, keeping his eyes on him at the window. As his wife joined him the child high up on the wobbling pole began crying. She quickly turned, unable to keep looking.

After several months as things became worse she suddenly loved everything about Bombay, about being in India, an excessive love, even loving what was bad.

From the apartment at 42A Nepean Sea Road on one side were the rocks and the Arabian Sea, on the other side the Russian consulate, where there was only occasional movement.

In India he was more than an ocean away from politics, the protests over Vietnam. It was happening elsewhere. And there was enough around him without him worrying about elsewhere. He felt separate, even if temporarily, from his own country. Hippies from America and Europe strolled along the streets, having rejected their own civilisations. Some sat cross-legged in the sun outside temples, expecting Indians to give alms as they left. Australians and Swiss were among them. The contrast between well-off Indians and the poor, the very poor, and the extent of the poverty and the illnesses, became a daily buffeting. It forced him to ask if socialism was an answer. Because of the scenes surrounding him he couldn't help looking about for possible solutions. The blurriness of "socialism" was one of the attractions, broad enough to reduce every disadvantage. The word itself was ready to take on the task. He continued working in the office.

Indian women, their calm attentiveness. So he talked more. And in two years he hardly drank, only the occasional glass of Indian beer.

The Rhine, another mighty river had gouged itself into the earth.

Tennis court ankle deep in snow, Grenoble.

'I can explain everything,' looking over her shoulder.

In the leper colony the director seated in his office stressed to him that leprosy was not a virus, it was transmitted by touch. Outside men and women could be seen lying on the ground or sitting on benches, their faces and limbs disfigured. A nail can be passed through a leper's hand, the director explained, and he will not feel it. Here was a man who chose to spend his days behind walls among people disfigured and dying from a disease that was transmitted by touch. Then and later it did present the question: would such a close proximity add to kindness, wisdom? Behind his desk the director in a white shirt was easygoing, almost bureaucratic. He was virtually anonymous. As he continued talking, a leper in khaki shorts entered with cups of tea. These he passed around one at a time, held between the stumps of both hands. The director had been impressive for being matter-of-fact. Now he too is dead, gone in the way of the many limbs and faces of the lepers he served.

It felt like the beginning of experience. It was more direct than bookish knowledge or what was acquired through film and news reports, which perhaps was no experience at all.

He had nothing that could be called political experience.

Above the regular sounds of traffic, the penetrating car and scooter horns, cries of people selling small items—the daily racket of survival—it was the harsh calls of the crows sitting in trees that made the most memorable sound in the leper colony, and all other parts of the city. At Calcutta airport he bought Che Guevara's diaries, and later Cohn-Bendit's 'left-wing alternative', without bothering to read what had been written before them. Somehow these books were associated with crowds. And yet he felt there was nothing in them which related to the India before him.

When he fell on the icy street in Darjeeling, local people rushed forward and helped him to his feet; the extra concern of people living at high altitude.

Beginnings he has remembered:

A cart drove between the two big stringybarks and stopped.

Travel and travellers are two things I loathe—and yet here I am, all set to tell the story of my expeditions.

For a long time I used to go to bed early.

There is a spectre haunting Europe, the spectre of…

A wise man once said that next to losing its mother, there is nothing more healthy for a child than to lose its father.

Gentlemen, start your engines.

There is nobody less suited than I am to start talking about memory.

As Gregor Samsa awoke one morning from uneasy dreams he found himself transformed in his bed into a gigantic insect.

For a while, she wasn't sure her husband was her husband, much as, when you're dozing, you're not sure whether you're thinking or dreaming, whether you're actually in charge of your own thoughts or have completely lost track of them out of sheer exhaustion.

And others almost forgotten.

When wading out in the mangroves for the ferry at a

fishing village called Gorai north of Bombay, she pointed to yellow fish swirling around their ankles. Looking down he saw they were water snakes. Somehow she leapt and balanced on his head, while his feet began tilting and sinking into the mud. Then the curious feeling of having survived—survived something minor. Earlier they saw the flash of iridescent blue of a kingfisher skimming over the beach.

He definitely remembers arriving home from school and taking the Nestlé condensed milk from the pantry, and next day went to do it again only to find it swarming with ants. There was his increasing interest in clammy girls as they began standing nearby, first observing them, how they were different in many small ways, and then treating them with calculated indifference, cousins who paid attention to him, and were feeling just as experimental, and the Stewart girls up the street. Overall was a general acceptance of ordinariness. Wages were low. There were no supermarkets. To travel overseas required regular saving the way couples did for their first home. Hot days (Adelaide) didn't bother him. Admiral butterflies in the bushes. And the happiness of his young wife, which he had never seen in anyone before and gave him the feeling of being above all others, chosen and elevated for a specific purpose. He wondered whether women showed happiness more. Did they experience more happiness than men?

His efforts to be individual were too deliberate and made him unpleasant.

Throughout that time in Bombay, black-and-white images continued from Vietnam. All photographs indicated humidity and perspiration, soldiers surrounded by a terrain and a mostly impassive people who could not be trusted. The bewildered sunken eyes typical of soldiers in war, here mostly American, looked at the camera more bewildered than expected. His younger brother had been in the first conscription from South Australia, and no-one knew exactly where in Vietnam he was. He was over there when their father who disapproved of the war died unexpectedly. Very few Indians they met regularly in Bombay approved of America's action, and already some doubted whether technology, America's "firepower", was a superiority that could overwhelm Asian patience—although he barely discussed the war at all. News from other places arrived via magazines weeks after it had happened. It hardly mattered. India close up was crowded with complexities which required an almost daily reaction, more than enough to fill his thoughts.

Noises, colours, shapes of bodies have more or less remained. The pavement-dwellers asleep under white sheets formed landscapes in miniature, bare hills and valleys of raised knees. Ringing of small bells coming out of the side-street temple; very common. Walls and the inside of certain shops, etc. were painted a glossy green. Others pale blue. Buses with dozens of large and small dents and hub caps missing still managed to keep going forward and stopping at set intervals. Combined with the unusual colour of walls produced a faint homesickness. Often the sight of something prompted a comparison. In Afghanistan, where he first became ill, the colour was mud-ochre and lapis lazuli. The austere landscape and its people wrapped in layers of cloth, the men in Kabul and in the villages strolling about carrying long, inlaid rifles, gave the feeling he really was at the outer frontier. These silent figures appeared as figures separate from the world as he knew it. But behind the counter in the cheap hotel, Kabul, there was the man with a small head who kept shrugging with intricate politeness, his many subtle and not so subtle types of shrugging multiplied his appeal.

While the face long ago faded it is the virtuoso shrugging that has kept him alive, and quite possibly over the years the many small shoulder movements have become exaggerated. Wherever he went nothing matched what he had imagined, not exactly.

They looked around at other couples and saw they were similarly at ease. Of a friend who had put on weight it was 'because she is happy'. An exception was the Englishwoman in Bombay whose husband from Leeds had moved in with a Punjabi woman. Finding out where they lived she stood in the street and screamed and yelled up at them, heaping curses on the young woman. It's all she could talk about. In her apartment, which still had traces of her husband, he listened to the details of their marriage, how she hadn't noticed any change in him, and the daily confusions of living in a foreign place which she found unsettling. She would have to go back to Britain. She asked where had she gone wrong. Her husband didn't know what he was doing. If she waited he might come back. As she tore into the appearance and devious personality of the younger woman blotches appeared on her face. It was hard to imagine a husband coming back to her. The Punjabi woman offered infinitely more mystery with her voice, eyes and skin, all the way down to her feet. As well there was an element of plunder in having her. He could see the Englishman would not return to this angry, plain woman, and after he wondered if that were a possibility she stood up suddenly and they never saw each other again. The extreme attentiveness of Indian women and their interest in western habits, although often westernised themselves, produced an array of persistent temptations.

Absorbed as he was in the India which surrounded him a feeling had taken hold of the danger of missing westernness, its language, habits and traditions, which formed a large part of him. And the separation from his own country where he grew up and had family seemed to widen by the day. If he didn't leave India and rejoin his westernness by going home or elsewhere he would soon be lost, forgotten at home and anywhere else western. Yet if he stayed in India he would remain always outside, with nothing underfoot. He felt out of place; neither here nor there. At the same time the enormous numbers of people crowding the cities and villages of India rendered him insignificant. He was merely one anonymous figure among the hundreds of millions. A similar uncomfortable realisation had occurred later in Rome. Wherever the eye settled there was evidence of the efforts of an industrious people who had long ago lived and worked, their achievements scattered all around him in the form of temples and fountains, and other buildings still standing, and broken columns and carved stone left lying on the ground. It made him feel—it was apprehension—that whoever he was or whatever he did was of no significance. Later he was told George Eliot said something similar, although she would not have been killed, as he almost was, brushed by a speeding bus while crossing an empty street below on the left of the Steps to get the morning's paper.

Not a specific occasion remains of the mysterious extreme pleasure, not the hopeless first attempt of entry ('put it down to experience'), nor the last nor those in between, including the part-attempts. How or where it took place is hardly remembered, more a melting into one another. Some names have gone. Always retained though is what had been allowed by the woman: given on trust, spreading to gratitude, which for him only increased the power of the moment. And their gentle, washed-over expression afterwards. It is possible that the withholding required of the successful male establishes a withholding of emotions in everyday life. Among themselves men rarely talked about women and sex, keeping anything they knew about it to themselves. By his fifties he noticed such talk had petered out altogether. Occasionally a coarse joke might be told where the man comes off second-best.

For a long time the church was the tallest building in a city or town. Strange disappointment in Spain and Italy at the loudspeakers fitted alongside church bells to give a greater volume to the ringing.

Two old men on a park bench, London, slapping their knees laughing.

Book knowledge accumulated at a methodical rate, giving the illusion it was adding to experience.

Much later he realised his reading was not really reading. It was accumulating pages, without fully entering the words and sentences.

The morning they left Bombay was watery, brown, the streets and roads awash from the monsoon, and the road to the airport flooded. Chaotic scenes inside the terminal involving saturated people.

For him views presented by nature were more clearly remembered than the behaviour between people, the one being stationary and having an apparent simplicity. Snow-white peaks in the Himalayas lit up one by one by the rising sun, as if someone was pulling a switch. Others too in the jeep gasped when Mt Everest in the distance was pointed out. From an immense squat base taking shape as the mist lifted, Kangchenjunga appeared as if just down the end of the main street, Darjeeling. Pale brown sand of the Sahara, circular patterns of. Empty side street, early morning—Paris. Those rivers in flood—always worth seeing. The way elephants move very slowly, methodically, through the bush. Inconspicuous beginnings of rivers before they become broad rivers. Black seas and violent racing foam in the Southern Ocean, even larger waves approaching at an angle in threes. Aside from anything else, our ability to traverse at will what lies between land is an impressive human achievement, using 'the watery part of the world'. July, 1969, a man stood on the moon and tottered about. Anyone born after would look at the moon differently from those born before the pictures made a fact of the landing.

They attended weddings and funerals in India.

Invited to dinner, it was wise to have a snack first: only after ten p.m. would the dishes be served. How different habits can appear peculiar. A few hours from Bombay at a farm set up to help blind people find work he met a man who although blind had jumped into a well to save a young woman. In the train on the way back an exceptionally neat young blind man in a crisp white shirt had an alarming ability to reel off statistics of Test cricket and looked into the distance as if seeing them as remembered. In their small rooms many of these people had still placed posters of Hindu gods on the wall, although they could not see them.

He wrote aerogrammes to his mother downplaying the discomfort. Partly out of superiority, also to position himself that he was not simply another Australian in London, he tried describing to people he met some of the extremes of living in a hot confusing country, how India had few of the conveniences of Europe and where there were extraordinary sights to be seen only there. He even liked to show he had superior knowledge of Indian food. After all, he had lived over there. But it seemed that India had already entered and passed through the British. It was hardly a new or unfamiliar subject, not even a particularly interesting one, rather it was part of them, of their past, of what contributed to what they now were and how they regarded the rest of the world. It reminded him of the white sheets over the people who slept on the pavements in Bombay, how the raised knee within gave shape to a landscape. He had written in a notebook, '...the slimy track made by the snail of history' —Robert Musil. At Amritsar the small enclosed square where Colonel Dwyer gave the order to fire on the crowd, killing more than 370, the marks on the wall were framed in cheap wood, 'British bullet here'. In Berkeley Square, where he had found work, a blue plaque on a wall identified the house where Clive of India had lived.

To be admitted (amoebic dysentery) to the Tropical Diseases Hospital at St Pancras drew attention to his experiences and gave him a suffering superiority. At ten in the morning figures emerged to gather in the corridor around the tea urn, shoes in the shape of boats, Indian 'bush shirts', embroidered slippers, Kolhapuri chappals, as if they were still in the hot countries they had been working in. Here were people who had similar experiences to his. Together they spoke easily and knowingly, the tea-planter from Assam who thought that while he was in town he'd look for a wife, the tall man who visited underdeveloped countries for Crown Agents, the missionary who'd picked up a skin disease in a remote part of Africa, a guard from the British Museum who had caught something behind the lines in Burma during the war. There was a middle-aged schoolteacher from Uganda ('it is God's country') who had worms and vomited in the basin, and a nun who'd been bitten by a rabid dog in Biafra. In the far bed, a handsome man from Mali said he was writing a novel in his language, not French. Wearing strange clothing adopted from others, they appeared as figures to one side, left over from an imperial past. With one of them he'd stand in pyjamas at the window and look down at the railway yards of St Pancras Station. There was always something to see, constant movement, while the man standing beside him went on reminiscing about parts of India or Africa. It was a broad expanse of tracks just below, and well into the night they could hear the shunting and bang-rattle of trains and wagons which began again early in the morning. It had been Apu's view of the railway tracks in Satyajit Ray's film that had prompted him to go and live in India, and in an ungainly piece of symmetry there he was looking down at railway tracks from a hospital where he had been admitted because of his time in India, and Afghanistan.

The taste of figs picked from the tree at home, Adelaide. Where the house stood had once been an orchard. They kept fowls in the corner behind wire netting; not unusual—roosters crowed from other backyards at all hours. It was one of the first houses in the street to install a Hills Hoist clothes line. Some of his relatives had Reader's Digest condensed books arranged on their shelves, the maroon spines with gold lettering calculated to make them feel learned. When his father was in a rush at breakfast he drank his tea from the saucer. Children with polio lay horizontally on frames to straighten their bodies and could be seen on the footpath outside their houses. There was one living opposite. He was called Andrew. Long lines of fire and smoke along the Hills facing the house, ash falling on their shoulders and the front lawn, Black Friday. People he had got to know in India visited him in London.

At a polling station in the Melbourne Town Hall where he had taken a job he met Arthur Calwell who was voting in the federal election. With his hat in one hand, a shoelace undone, he was about to lose. The difficulty of having hopes and trying to convince others of them would be a wear on the spirit. Only a rare personality—possibly one disordered—would immerse themselves in politics to that extent, to absorb over many months and years the defeats, while always keeping one eye on the majority. In the Seventies and later when he met at various times other leaders, Fraser, Whitlam—his vanity was parochial—Keating and Malcolm Turnbull, each displayed, in different degrees, an absence. While talking to a single person they seemed to continue to address a wider audience of many hundreds of thousands somewhere else. They had become practised at saying one thing, at the same saying something entirely different! Listening to them it became a matter of waiting for the real person: they had become many different people. He preferred the more direct, enquiring manner of Pierre Ryckmans, Anita Brookner, Fred Williams, all no longer alive, and Helen Garner. Over many years they had worked hard at their lives to give shape to their thoughts and express them into what would remain theirs alone.

Abruptly and against his will he turned to political theory. The absorbing nearness of India constantly demanded an opinion, preferably one with some sort of historical basis and easily defended. India had offered itself as part-feudal, part-infant-industrial, and a mixture of Hindu and Muslim layerings, a general congestion, chaos made more intractable by cows wandering the streets, the many different languages and dialects. The daily contrast between beggars alongside people being driven about in cars, hutments made out of tin and cardboard against the walls of mansions, figures in filthy ragged clothing brushing past silken saris, and naked children with distended stomachs or others with a grotesque infection of an eye—all was enough for him to turn to "socialism" as a solution. At night around the Flora Fountain children did their homework under the streetlights. It was as if examples of inequality were being paraded to point to socialism as the most obvious and necessary answer, although it was not fully clear to him how much it could do. The Indians themselves seemed to accept the contrasts, some shrugging. And although he had learned to talk easily about capital, surplus value, communism and so on, he indulged in some shrugging of his own. The plight of people on the streets—and in the villages and out in the fields—was constantly visual. It was not happening to him. All he could do was apply to it the theories of others and would never know if they fitted.

In London in the Seventies he tried to avoid any reference to 'class' in his thinking and certainly in conversation (the main reason he found English novels stale, preferring for a time to enjoy the fresh air of American fiction). As with the layers of poverty visible in Asia, signs of class across London appeared as exaggerated Englishness, allowing those at the higher level to make confident use of it, the Rolls-Royce waiting outside a club. If a prime minister—or any man or woman—opened their mouth the accent identified their origins, their class, as did the sort of trousers they wore. The almost comical air of superiority of the English. The air of indifference was made more so by their oblique way of talking. Below them the Cockneys, Scots and others got on with it, tough, and the young women were playful. There were rows of men sleeping under the arches of Charing Cross Bridge. At the office, men in all seriousness beckoned him by his surname. English pop groups were a theatrical success. Their clothing and behaviour were chosen as protest against their elders, against any acceptance of class; many were Cockney or from Liverpool, happier to flaunt it than hide it. Fashion was given the name Carnaby Street. Much of it was instinctively youthful: if they used the

Union Jack in any way it was for mockery. Otherwise the English excelled at supplying the needs of men, it was a male culture. Men were comfortable in the company only of men, and so there were the clubs behind the Ritz and along the Mall—the chandeliers and the back of an armchair could be seen from the street. And the English were excellent at producing men's shirts, men's shoes, and making the best fishing rods, and supplying the best in gun shops, cigar stores and the wine merchants.

It was difficult to ignore the sullen dissatisfaction of what was still being called the 'working class'. At intervals and increasingly in the Seventies there were strikes by the garbage collectors, bus drivers, hospital staff and bakers; trains were far from running on time. Typesetters refused to set editorials their union disagreed with, leaving blank spaces in the newspapers which suddenly appeared as an assault on all that was tolerant, the best of British values. The coalminers' strike in 1972 seemed to bring together strands of the general mood, for there was the common image of the miner's dirty dangerous work and the meal being served on a kitchen table by the miner's grim wife. Common decency said the cause had to be right. On a Sunday afternoon he joined the several thousand supporters in Trafalgar Square and listened to the strike leaders, small figures in the mid-distance taking turns to shout into a microphone. The urgent tone of the speakers made him look around and ask whether if the strike was about to be successful such a gathering would hardly be necessary. Numbers were required for pictorial purposes; but an implacable arithmetic stood in the way. The crowd filling the square on Sunday were supporters, some carrying banners. When they left they had contented expressions. And he stood as a bystander at the edges. He could have been a tourist pausing before moving on. It took six weeks for Edward Heath to outlast Arthur Scargill.

On a back road north-east of Madrid they passed a man accompanying a donkey, and to save on leather he had his shoes strung around his neck and was walking with bare feet. The Spanish Civil War and Spain and its countryside did not fail to move him. Looking up in Teruel and in villages he could see windows surrounded by bullet marks. Certain beliefs if followed could reach an ultimate seriousness. The repressed atmosphere of the villages; not a good atmosphere, not sufficiently human. And he wondered whether the villages would be much different had the Republicans won.

Printed sign on manager's desk at first job interview, Adelaide: 'Before You Louse Things Up—THIMK!' Also on the desk a large ashtray made out of a tan boxing glove. Silly things are remembered more clearly than serious ones. Bantam rooster on the stool in the kitchen repeatedly crowing which had the whole family crying with laughter, including their father. Squatting to catch tadpoles in the creek and bringing them home in a jar.

How many people nearby, such as uncles and aunts, the teachers at school, appeared to be old people, yet were barely in their forties.

Often the sight of something introduced a comparison.

English people standing beside him in trains and lifts, at shop counters, and coming towards or passing alongside on the street. They spoke English, but it was different to him. They said 'indeed'. Out of caution they had constructed a view of the world around the meaning and non-meaning of 'indeed'. The friend from Brisbane who had taken the train to Birmingham in the hope of getting a job at the Dunlop factory was told it was throwing tyres onto a truck—'Well, what experience do you have?' The way when introduced to a certain kind of Englishman they would say, 'Ah, yes, Donald Bradman.' Or, 'Where did you say you were from again?'

Instead of the green rectangles of southern England, it was the uncultivated parts of Scotland and Yorkshire that appealed to him. At the same time it felt strange standing on that part of the earth—even to the extent of wondering what he was doing there. He had grown his hair longer, always reading, almost systemically. By finishing one book, then picking up another, he was all too conscious of it adding another layer to what he knew, a reinforcement, which also happened when he saw another important art exhibition, of which he saw as many as possible. His wife said he was slouching more. With the Muslim woman walking on the beach in darkness out of Bombay, brushing against her while talking, moving, about to move his arm again, before hesitating. In London he saw a eucalyptus in the corner of a friend's back garden and began seeing them in the most unlikely places.

'I'd like you to meet my eldest. He has a big mouth like his father.'

Sometimes Australia appeared as rocks.

She, who kept talking throughout in a perfunctory sort of way.

Facing him while removing her clothes.

Economics and systems of government had dwindled to almost nothing, only a vague interest flickered at the edges—anything to avoid a feeling of futility. More for general interest than to examine the situation, they went to the Soviet Union in winter 1974. Often his attraction to cities and landscapes was first prompted by novels. And not many other people had been to Russia. His wife was nervous about going. A few days before, Solzhenitsyn had been sent into exile. At Yasnaya Polyana the curator with the wide apart eyes and wild laugh, Tanya, who was in love with Tolstoy. The sight of the enormous sofa in his workroom. In his Moscow townhouse we shook our heads in admiration at the stuffed bear holding a tray at the foot of the stairs, said to be the one Tolstoy strangled with his bare hands when it attacked him in a forest. How the cold has shaped the Russian mind. At the Leningrad

Chess Club he played a game. After what seemed only a few minutes he lost. Always difficult reading someone's face in a country where English was not spoken, such as Japan, Russia. Condoms suspended in the ice of the Neva, each one preserving a story.

He still talked about Trotsky, a young man's figure, and the ten million words Lenin reputedly had written (he had read very few of them). Enough of politics in theory and practice had been absorbed and become part of him, so he thought. Whereas the worlds presented by Turgenev, Tolstoy, Chekhov, Lermontov, Mandelstam continued, without effort, to increase their hold.

The basement flat in Langham Street behind the BBC where he would be interviewed twenty-seven years later was neat but permanently dark. It added to the feeling of disappearing from view. In London as in Bombay there were no family meals, which were both exasperating and enjoyable. His wife was missing her parents. Her father would interrupt a conversation by putting a transistor to his ear to listen to the races. Reading the novel he had written each morning in Bombay he could see it was false, it had no natural basis, there was no reason for it, and after attempts at revision in the basement flat he dismantled it and put the pages out with the rubbish. Whenever he looked up through the iron railings he could see the bins on the pavement, a good enough reason to move after a year to Notting Hill, then to Royal Crescent in Holland Park, where there was light. The *Times Literary Supplement* over the telephone giving him a first book to review: 'We only have one rule here. We would rather you didn't use the pronoun "I".' Reading the Sunday papers and coming across unusual information: soldiers in war, according to Ernst Jünger, destroy musical instruments but preserve mirrors.

Going to Belfast and later to West Africa and Borneo, etc. were adventures from ordinariness. To a visitor unaccustomed to it, Belfast had every appearance of dangerous; to people living there the dangers were more an everyday nuisance to be endured. Without warning, armoured cars mounted the pavements. Always the possibility of bombs. Police stations and courthouses were enclosed in wire netting, looking like aviaries, and to enter a bar on the Falls Road was to first crawl through a netting maze, there as an obstacle to bombers. Alone with danger or at least discomfort was something he didn't normally experience. Wondering whether it made any difference, if it had any effect on him, he looked instead at the figures on the street and was left with respect for their weary stoicism. This too became part of his worldliness. In London there were jokes about the Irish, usually shown as hapless, and there was a widespread wariness of the French, made acceptable by wryness or exaggeration, and they enjoyed mocking the Germans, all of which entered comedy sketches and commercials on television. After many years of stop-and-start trying and being vetoed by de Gaulle, Britain in 1973 joined the European Union. They read the *Guardian*, the *New Yorker*, *Paris Review*. The novels they talked about were Michel Tournier's *The Erl-King*, John Berger's *G*. They had the highest regard for Borges; Donald Barthelme, Robbe-Grillet, Günter Grass, Musil and Márquez were also seen as antidotes to English realism. They read *The Female Eunuch* with curiosity, more interested in fiction. By making himself understood in London his voice had crept into being an English voice. Looked in on Lord Denning at the Court of Appeal, an alert figure with a small fixed smile. While the images of many hundreds of people going about their work have disappeared, the figure of Denning dispensing justice in court has remained. Richard Burton's tomb behind a church at Mortlake was a tent in heavy

Carrara marble, an immediate contradiction, and the Islamic star dominated by a crucifix placed there by his wife. With increasing momentum he said yes to virtually everything. Agreeing to participate in Joseph Beuys' blackboard performance at the ICA, Beuys a highly intelligent shaman in odd modern clothing, made more memorable still by the remains of a Second World War face. Standing alongside as Beuys wrote words in chalk he was expected to make intelligent comments which Beuys listened to politely before dropping each blackboard to the floor where a young assistant would step forward and spray fixer to preserve them. It was Beuys who said, 'Gentleness, Indirectness, Imperceptibility, and often "Anti-technics" are my choices.' At other times they went to lectures of high quality by Borges, Ivan Illich and George Steiner; all no longer alive. Such a large city could offer depth in concentrated areas, even if the numbers at the ICA were small.

So comprehensive and well written were the British newspapers they provided the illusion he was close to events, even closely involved in a detailed sense. Very little happened in faraway Australia. It didn't get into the papers, the rest of the world not interested. There was a war in Biafra and problems in the Middle East.

Otherwise the grainy photographs and stories concerned Britain and Europe. And the United States. There was always something happening there. At the news that Patrick White had won the Nobel Prize for Literature he and others went about triumphant, and the importance of Great Britain and European receded, if briefly.

Not having children allowed them to move about with ease. As years passed they were left more to themselves, and saw in each other limitations. Despite their affection, habits assumed to be harmless became irritations.

On the tarmac at Perth airport he noticed something he had missed for the past five years: a land breeze. It was a novelty to the English people who had also stepped off the plane. They had paid ten pounds to be flown to Australia as migrants. Now they stood gazing up at the vast southern-hemisphere sky where there was not a single cloud. They had never encountered such enormousness, along with it a feeling of emptiness, and they went quiet. All around was pale khaki, no green. Their confused impressions were eased by the land breeze. Gough Whitlam was the new prime minister, and writers and artists were welcomed back. Attending universities became free. Early in the morning from a terrace house someone's pet galah or white cockatoo, at that stage he couldn't tell the difference, began screeching, a noise peculiarly appropriate to inner Sydney. It went with the scrappy faded paintwork of the houses, the iron lace and humidity. There was certainly a mood of informality. An editor of a literary magazine dropped in wearing shorts to collect some pages. Men and women wore Levi's and T-shirts, and women put on overalls normally worn by men, although some chose pink. For them feminism was visual too. If they had a car it was okay to let it appear run-down.

Poetry readings in pubs were popular. Someone had the idea of printing short stories on newsprint and inserting them in newspapers. Anthologies and essays came out. After a story appeared in the *New Yorker* a poet and his girlfriend stood outside his house and sang praises in verse. Anything felt possible. The mood was exaggerated by a localised energy. There was the feeling he could contribute to a literary culture which was still being formed, something that was hardly possible in the Old World. They understood Patrick White's complaint of the surrounding 'dreary, dun-coloured realism'. Novels required a distortion, almost a matter of being deliberately different—yet somehow without strain. Initially it would be done via the short story. The idea of making a living seemed far-fetched. Every other writer had a grant from the government, some yet to be published. To be separate from everybody else, avoiding the Sydney lunch, to be austere and pure, following the example of Flaubert, he had no telephone, no television, not even a watch. Instead of extra clarity it only made him cold; he could feel it. He continued working in the mornings without interruption.

She crossed the street and came into his apartment wearing nothing under her clothes. It made him feel special.

And the hospital in Zanzibar with rows of figures under mosquito nets, some with large stains of blood. Between the beds and under them lay other patients, late arrivals or less-urgent cases, making it difficult for doctors and others to reach the beds. The silence of the patients: the patience of the sick and dying. Livingstone followed by Stanley set out on their explorations from Zanzibar. In a cafe in Sydney he met a man called Livingstone whose Christian name was Stanley. There were the luxuriant trees which grew cloves, women drying them on blankets on the ground which gave the air a pleasant aroma, an altogether humble source for the small black cloves which travelled long distances to flavour his mother's stewed-apple desserts in Adelaide, done better by his first wife in Melbourne. It was not the trees and the cloves arranged on the ground he returned to, but the figures in rows inside the hospital. The glaring white sand. Was it white—as white as all that? Lying on the hospital floor alongside his mother the boy turned and tried a smile out of uncertainty, the smile held, when around him everyone remained expressionless.

It certainly feels like being below towards the bottom of the earth, which has been populated and built upon, where people live and move about mostly contented.

Those accustomed to the stars still find themselves pausing and looking up at them, so many fill the night sky there's hardly room for more. There are more stars here than in the northern hemisphere. The light of day is brighter too, a pitiless light, giving objects sharp edges, shadows angled black. Faces have kept on developing a national squint. The light which can be blazing has made opinions straightforward, without shading. The characters in novels tend to be plain and the films brightly lit, both in acting and actual lighting. Even in summer the light in Europe is noticeably softer. The air in Europe is soft too, making the edges of things blurry. The imprecision is a more accurate way of reading the world, where beginning with language nothing is fixed or brightly lit. The blurriness of the natural world helped the Impressionists too: the work had already been done for them.

The small hotel near the Pompidou Centre where she gave a hoarse cry like some sort of helpless animal.

Instead of toilet paper, newspaper torn into squares hung on nails or with string. By coincidence toilet paper rolls arrived when the lavatories moved indoors.

On the roof of the mud mosque, Timbuktu, as the muezzin in purple robe began licking his fleshy lips in preparation for midday prayers. The memory is clear of being invited to stand nearby and watch as he recited the sonorous melancholy of words which travel a long distance. Twenty-five years later in Aleppo outside the mosque near the covered market it was still more sonorous and affecting, although the muezzin was behind a wall hidden from view.

After his second marriage, the misery he left behind of the first.

How women lying in the bath called him in, where he could not help but appreciate their bodies.

An underlying instability—of becoming careless or deliberately offending someone in order to have them react, rejecting him. Dismissed from four jobs, the last one in London, after which a sense of freedom. He had developed a resistance to work that was not his own, and he was hardly a good worker. He would have appeared uncooperative to those trying to work with him. An indifferent manner was made even worse by being reminded of his own inaction. If he had remained one more day in London he would stay where he didn't belong, for the rest of his life.

In Sydney he went from apartment living to a house in Spring Street, Birchgrove, another house at 47 Darling Street, to an apartment in Chippendale, then another, and finally to 42 Macleay Street in Potts Point, where for nineteen years he has remained (seated, recalling memories). If there was a disturbance in the morning while he was working, even a squeaking floorboard, he would yell out with indignation. Irritability felt like resistance—to what he was not sure. By being pure he had the obscure feeling he was doing something distinctive and worthwhile.

Although evenly spaced by divisions, time can be experienced differently in certain situations. It was common in India for a farmer catching a train at four p.m. to arrive at five a.m. and squat all day on the platform until it arrived; an ancient view of time: he might as well wait on the platform as do anything else. Opening a book borrowed from a great-aunt or elderly neighbour he would find a dried flower pressed between the pages, a practice related to a moment, a marker, enough for him to wonder what part of a woman's life it represented, replaced now by the less sentimental email or telephone call. He can almost feel the moment he strapped on his first watch, given by an uncle, which had pale green numerals visible in the dark, later said to be radioactive. For a while she kept photograph albums. She took colour photographs of people, of family and friends, all happy to be photographed, few if any photographs of buildings or trees. During the riot at the Test match in Bombay he watched the crowd below change shape as it stampeded into a corner. The irrational fluidity of a crowd—like a drop of mercury rolling on a table—was unpleasant to watch; he would remember this when reading Canetti's *Crowds and Power*. The reverse occurred in Calcutta as a curfew had the normally crowded streets empty of people and movement—which increased in him the not so pleasant feeling of individuality. Visiting London she took her camera to Kew, where she gave it to him to put around his neck, which he didn't want. How an ordinary enough moment is looked back upon as the beginning of other dissatisfactions. The fax machine arrived. It could be heard rolling out pages in the middle the night. Placed in prominent positions it was a notable addition to a household, and those who hadn't yet acquired one were regarded with surprise. What a fax machine could instantly deliver did seem remarkable. Yet it too didn't last. In a little over five years the internet followed by the mobile phone came to dominate their lives. There was a compression of advances in technology. Hi-fi systems and speakers costing thousands actually gave the "perfect" sound. At every opportunity robots replaced workers on the assembly line, and computers proceeded narrowly to beat Grand Masters. The fax machine, the Adler semi-portable typewriter and bulky black telephone on the desk were thrown out. A transformation of society had taken place, one of those influential moments, and the speed of change was accepted without surprise.

The mobile phone introduced a release of words in public, the most intimate conversations in buses and trains and on the pavement whispered audibly or spoken loudly and rapidly. Nothing like it had happened before. Along with the tasks made convenient by the computer the very small telephone in the palm of the hand although aural and mechanistic represented a change to society as wide-reaching as the pill, while the pill was soft and worked in the depths of privacy.

In his kitchen in Chicago, 1973, Nelson Algren said the cafes in Paris lit up when Sartre walked in. He didn't want to talk about Simone de Beauvoir. 'She used me.' Presumably he meant in *The Mandarins* where he is recognisable and transformed into art, whereas Algren's novels rely less on transformation, more on what he would regard as a greater imagination. In contrast to Anglo-Saxon societies a writer in France is assigned a high position. Mitterrand would take time off to visit Michel Tournier at his house near Versailles. Streets and squares in Paris are named after philosophers, Foucault and Barthes only the most recent ones. Philosophy is taught from the age of fifteen at schools. Seventy thousand people followed Sartre's hearse to Montparnasse cemetery, 1980. Now that they have died only their contributions remain: Beckett, Marguerite Yourcenar, Doris Lessing, V. S. Naipaul, Thomas Bernhard, Christina Stead, Patrick White, Borges, Tournier, Sartre. And more.

At some stage men began wearing baseball caps instead of the usual hats or no hats at all. A delegation of farmers must have gone to the Midwest of America. They would have brought some home as souvenirs the way others return with photographs. The baseball cap proved to be practical, easier to wear inside the cab of a tractor and could be stuffed in the back pocket. It's now a common sight on the heads of farmers as well as elderly men in the cities, some wearing bermuda shorts and long white socks, following their wives like large children. The cap is now part of the police uniform. Soldiers too have it on their heads. It was natural for the president of the United States to put one on whenever possible. Our own prime minister has been quick to place one firmly on his head whenever he stepped outside Canberra. Some women looked racy wearing the cap. In the American cities rappers and young men took to wearing them back to front, and it appeared like that in American television series, a fashion quickly followed by top tennis players. In no time at all reversing the cap became widespread locally. Adding to this appearance of youth and energy was the wearing of sneakers or runners. It was democratic and androgynous: just as many women as men went about in the same sneakers. And early in the morning or at lunchtime in groups or singly they were out jogging or fast-walking along the pavements and in the parks, even in the Botanical Gardens, brushing past people out to enjoy the flowers or ordinary pedestrians on the street, a craze for physical fitness which had become widespread and required special footwear.

Slightly plump short-haired blonde on the back seat of the family Ford Zephyr, Adelaide, her father owned and raced trotters. It was not the mostly bare body he remembers, but her girlfriend's view of him: 'he's an excuse for a man.' In the front garden: HORSE MANURE FOR SALE.

At Mopti the dust storm reaching the river, caramel-brown billowing, about to engulf the town as people looked on.

He was given the Christian name of his father's younger brother who was killed at the age of twenty-one falling from a horse as he jumped a fence near Bordertown, and somehow this remained a gap in his life. His father never spoke about him. No photograph is available to show he had existed, briefly.

It was a therapeutic culture. In Melbourne in the Eighties she had gone into therapy, as did her sisters and women friends. Each was fierce in defence of their therapist but not of their father. Some of his wife's friends were therapists or were training to be. They were the new priests, listening to confessions, remaining impassive at the most intimate thoughts, as expressed. Arriving in Sydney she needed the release of talking again across a room and every Tuesday went to a therapist recommended by others. When he returned from being away at sea she was not on the wharf down at Botany Bay, preferring to keep the meeting with the therapist. Very few men but many women had 'seen someone' or were wondering aloud whether they should or not. The therapy experience flowed into everyday life, where its terms had been picked up and easily digested—'But that's projection!'—all the way to newspaper columns, magazines, comedians, television documentaries. At approximately the same time, others were attracted to yoga, or to eastern religions and meditation, in a bid to achieve the serenity which had perhaps once been supplied by the churches, and for more rapid answers, a few turned to the ease of astrology.

These stood in the background the way billboards are spaced at intervals on busy streets offering soft certainties for personal needs, useful to some but an area he felt no need to enter. Besides, just as his father avoided identifying himself in captions under his photos, preferring '?' written in ink, which only drew more attention, he could not imagine talking about himself for fifty minutes once a week.

After interminable hesitation on his part it was the tall woman who took the initiative and led him up the stairs, twirling a high-heel sandal on a finger—theatrical and exaggerated, by just the right amount.

His first wife took secateurs and twisted and cut the ring off her finger, the second tugged and dug at her gold ring and threw it into the bin. The startling effect of the symbolism broken.

At intervals and without warning a feeling of perplexity: he could only just accept being alive. Seated at his desk or walking he would pause to wonder what he was doing there—on this particular patch of earth. Why should it be? Looking down he'd see his fingers, and see them move. Then further questions about this particular life—was he allowing it to shape itself? Did it need more from him?

The local barber who came on board the big ship at Port Said kept on clicking his scissors after he had finished, wanting to go on talking, explaining he wouldn't allow his daughter to marry a foreigner, including any European, pausing to look down at the activity on the wharf, still clicking his scissors. It had become a metallic tic. Nothing remains of his appearance and very little of what he said, only the sound of the scissors. Again, the visual oddness of what some people do to make a living.

They went looking for a house to buy and dutifully did. 'You've got to own in Sydney!' Turning a corner or at the end of a street the watery blue of the harbour leaked into the eye when least expected. A cream-painted ferry slid across like a 1950s kitchen cabinet. Cats, dogs, cockatoos and parrots, budgerigars, fish in tanks, occupied the houses of others. They too acquired a dog. An aerial view of the suburbs would show tennis courts and the pale blue of small swimming pools. Early in the morning the streets were wet as if watered by hand. Arguments over literature on back lawns almost turned into fist fights. It was the presence of the poets, including some from New Zealand, staking out their positions, dismissive of prose. Sometimes he could almost "see" the new literature, what could be the new way of writing, but it was in general and only fleeting. 'Did they stretch out on the couch?' 'No, stupid, that's analysis.' To be a fearless generaliser: follow the examples of Balzac, Tolstoy, Stendhal, etc. Looking up at the ceiling fan, Calcutta, the blades appeared to turn too slowly. Whenever he thought of his mother she was in her dressing gown in the kitchen. He was healthy and sleeping well even when the bus laboured up Darling Street outside their bedroom window. 'But that's a generalisation'—belonged to timid minds. Moving between fellow writers, family and others. 'Either I go now,' she said, undoing her dress, 'or I stay the night.' When he was young someone told him of a man who said he had sold sixty-eight insurance policies in a lunatic asylum. With her behind the hedge, Adelaide. The novel he wrote in Bombay he carried on as hand luggage, and once they had settled in London he began to read it. From the train the stony shape of Mont Sainte-Victoire appeared on the left as if covered in snow. How such a geological declaration patiently demanded to be painted, as a dog waits to be patted. Cézanne saw it and made it his own. He did not include the enormous crucifix which had been erected on its summit, an interference with what was natural. No other painter can now paint the mountain. Instead of seeing Mont Sainte-Victoire he now only sees one of

Cézanne's paintings of it.

As he grew older women became more interesting.

Even when resting at the wharf the vast container ship was never silent, always creaking.

As seen in Greece immediately after India, the west was where women allowed their breasts to move, to be seen to move. Tightly bound cultures where the very suggestion of breasts is avoided have the arranged marriages.

One divorce, followed ten years later by another. Using her knowledge of India she cooked curries, the quantities filling the bowls and the many side dishes were part of her abundance—her generosity. They formed an addiction to martinis. In its habits and comforts the marriage had become a marriage of regularity, with no surprise. After their separation she took him for his birthday to *Meistersinger*. This production was Germany's gift to Australia for its bicentenary, 1988. *Tosca* was the only other opera he had seen, and he had left at interval. He had shunned opera for being antique and exaggerated. Its artificiality was lush and represented all that his modernist instincts wanted to correct. It was also the province of ageing grandees, people who felt they should partake of culture and dressing up and stepping out to the opera did it. Its absurdity meant it didn't need to be taken seriously. And although *Meistersinger* was not one of Wagner's vicious deep-structured works with eventual death-worship, it unfolded that night with the depth of the oldest story in the world: a suitor has to pass a test for the hand of a daughter. No father however generous can be entirely approving of the man lying with his daughter night after night in marriage. The effect of this truth was given added power by the music. And that evening he could see a way forward, by going back—back towards the area of time-proven myth, but in a modern treatment. Within days he began his work. Later his second wife added to his interest in music. Haydn had been the composer his father concentrated on. Wagner had become his.

Wanting to know more about David Hume he picked up *My Own Life*. Aside from anything else, he admired Hume's steadiness. His autobiography began: 'It is difficult for a man to speak long about himself without vanity; therefore, I shall be short.' And finished with his life in a little under five pages.

In Melbourne he fell off a bike and cracked three ribs.

At the mortuary (Melbourne) he assumed an attitude of scientific enquiry as he looked down through the viewing window at the body laid out naked on a table. The pathologist stood next to the technician as he pulled the ribs apart, bending forward for leverage, and removed the heart and lungs, which he placed to one side. With hardly a pause he moved up to the head, and using an electric saw cut open the skull, lifted the brain out and put it on a silver tray. The man lying there had been in his late twenties, thin with long hair. It was an age he himself had sailed past, not noticing it, thirty years before. Life had gone from the young man who had overdosed, now just a body left behind. The technician and the pathologist both wearing white coats had worked methodically, removing the different parts which made up the whole.

Then the many more softer moments, almost daily. It could be a voice, a few words, or something seen or on a page, a change of weather, pleasures so recent and past they have scarcely registered.

The feeling of pleasure at stepping aside for another animal: the implacable yaks coming down on the same narrow path in the snow, Simla.

An emotional distance had hardened him unnecessarily. Finally he understood it to be a form of cheap protection.

He has tried to recall the distant relation in her late sixties who said while seated on the sofa she had two ambitions: to write a book and play the saxophone. And there is now no way of knowing whether she succeeded at either.

Self-appointed to "Boxing Correspondent" for a Sydney newspaper he occasionally went and took in the spectacle of two brightly lit men showing themselves in regulated rounds hitting one while themselves being hit, the shuffling and thudding, observing the difficulty of it all. The crowd too—people from somewhere else. Almost entirely men, seated in concentrated anticipation, a few women among them, good-time blondes down the front, all done up. Two handshakes. In 1993 when boxing returned to Madison Square Garden ('The World's Most Famous Arena') a sportswriter at ringside asked if he would like to meet Jake LaMotta who was in a suit climbing down from the ring after posing with other former champions, the tradition before a title fight. An even softer hand was felt in Sydney when George Foreman came up with his entourage to those seated ringside. 'Ev-nun, friend!' An exceptionally large soft right hand which went all the way back to the origins of boxing and so gave off a lethal impression of calm. These former champions have an afterlife in statistics and films, and the unexpectedly soft impression of their hands.

Usually it was his mother who phoned from Adelaide, for he never knew what to talk about. They both assumed an overlap of habits and memories—unsatisfactory, in some ways, like out-of-focus photographs. She believed they had more to talk about than they actually did. From a long distance he tried to take an interest. Living alone, she didn't appear to need any help. She didn't understand the way he lived, the work he did, and never asked; yet they continued naturally. 'All my children are clever.' Her life had been one of work using elbows and wrists, for a long time bent with none of the labour-saving devices, a washing machine or vacuum cleaner. It was pennies and shillings time, before decimal currency. Looking up from rolling pastry or rethreading the cord on a pair of pyjamas the small face was hoping to be amused. Family remained her most common subject and aside from one son her children had moved to other cities. 'Keep pulling that face and the wind might change and you'll be left stuck with it.' When she died suddenly a few days after he had listened to her on the telephone it was not a surprise but still a shock. Afterwards in the church hall where the tea urn and egg sandwiches and biscuits had been laid out he tried to suppress feelings of aloofness, of awkwardness at the relations advancing loudly to introduce themselves, their cheap suits and ties, the banal conversation of the minister with ginger hair holding the Good News Bible, the older women surveying him over their saucers, the drab ordinariness of the gathering. Even though most of them didn't go to church the decencies and limitations of Methodism were on display, as if nothing had changed since he had left home in a hurry almost forty years before—to become what? He disliked his reactions and stepped outside as soon as he could. It was not a close family, but now without both parents he was left alone.

As usual one of the large birds in the tree began calling the approach of dawn, answered by another from a distant tree. The world beginning all over again. Along with the spreading colours of dawn the wonder of it all!

The memories of Adelaide which appear ordinary remain stronger, more insistent than later more extreme experiences. And some things he was told of no apparent importance he cannot forget. 'The man knew all there was to know about poultry.'

The slight tufts of hair from her armpits, residue from the Seventies, for him the promise of unconventionality.

Their dismay at the Whitlam government as it fell apart. After many years of being denied power, once Labor was given power, it was as if the speed of the pent-up reforms, of seeing them enacted with ease—everything from recognising China to getting rid of university fees, tariffs and television licences, and divorce made easier—accelerated a mood of carelessness. A peculiar relaxation turned into self-importance and the rapid spending of money, the purchase of Jackson Pollock's *Blue Poles* held up as the epitome of extravagance. It continued. Each week exceeded the one before. A Middle Eastern financier appeared. There were dramas involving women. The faces of cabinet ministers perspired on television. It was all too human; it was hardly necessary to take an interest in what was happening in the rest of the world.

He was left asking whether he was part of the problem, that the elected government merely represented his own faults of unevenness, his underlying instability, mixed with an informality which came close to provincialism.

At least the economic sophistication of the Hawke–Keating years was a relief. As this took place various American presidents appeared on film in the distance and Margaret Thatcher was reshaping Britain.

From Bulawayo in the heat following the two prospectors in their Peugeot through thin trees and grey dust, stocky men in khaki shorts, born in Africa; the larger one from South Africa had married a Zimbabwean woman. Having lost their way they asked directions from a boy in a yellow boilersuit, guarding a group of women cutting branches. He was perhaps fourteen and held a Kalashnikov. Two soldiers in camouflage uniforms ran out from the trees on the right, big men who ordered them out and to stand against the back of the Peugeot. The danger of the moment showed when the women began backing away, the boy-soldier laughed, and the two prospectors speaking Swahili became servile. The soldiers and the fourteen-year-old marched them all for questioning to an army camp more than an hour away: olive-green tents above a khaki African river appeared. Here was experience he did not seek. It was true experience.

Two months passed away. First sentence of a chapter, Thomas Hardy.

Wine had replaced beer at an unexpected rate, even in country towns. Cars became longer, before becoming smaller. Country people began to say it was time the Melbourne Cup excluded foreign horses. As the ranks of marchers diminished on Anzac Day, the crowd looking on increased. The enormous quantity of wine and spirits taken over the years, the pleasure it has given, it has surely invaded his health. She liked to point out her stretch marks with a pensive pride. Peacocks in India moving slowly—antiquated-looking birds. 'I'm so hungry I could eat a baby through a cane chair'—according to an old soldier it was said during the war. She was small and never still, and had an emotional quick intensity. The enormous expanse of the Mississippi in flood. 'I did love you,' she said in a Canberra hospital before she died. The term 'love' made him pause seated by the bed, and pensive even now. Who was the married man who called his wife Bunny and his mistress Rabbit? It was someone he met or heard about in London. The friends who had begun dying before him, a few younger, others were more than seventy; one stabbed with a carving knife on the nature strip at dusk on St Kilda Road by a woman he had met a few weeks before in a psychiatric ward. Not all are remembered. Virtually all diminish into imprecision, or on unexpected occasions come partly forward. Nothing is finished. He was watching the man seated opposite who opened his mouth to hear better.

Considered objectively shoes are the strangest objects. Often he finds himself looking down at them. And hair. Now he needs a haircut only every three months, if that, and can get away with shaving every second day. At the same time—unless he was mistaken—his fingernails were growing at a faster rate and needed more regular trimming. It was too easy for his achievements in reading to exceed what he was doing working. After ten years the gradual then abrupt ending of the second marriage. Waking up while keeping his eyes closed, the sense of wonder and relief as a small part of him, eyelids, obeyed an instruction and lifted for him to see. The lack of vanity in animals. 'A culture that tries to skip philosophy will never grow up.' He allowed weak jokes, stories and facts to accumulate, while hoping to avoid the jokey informality which surrounded him.

The history of a single person surrounded by others.

Just when *nothing should surprise you* was accepted as necessary for worldliness, a friend telephoned in September telling him to switch on the TV—just as he did the second airliner hit at an angle the second tower. The collapse of one tower followed by its twin, and the curling wall of dust channelling up the street to overtake the fleeing crowd, made the special effects of the Hollywood disaster movies look manufactured. Almost immediately the Americans went into Afghanistan. At least one consequence was that ISIS set out on its conquests. The narrow cruelty of ISIS seemed to have a mediaeval aspect. V. S. Naipaul's they 'can fly a plane, but what they can't do is build one'—factual, was it reasonable? A minority within Islam who could no longer tolerate its impotence against the might of western technology, all that aluminium and free movement, borrowed the same technology to use against the west: computers, cell phones, airliners into tall buildings, videos (of beheadings), the roadside bombs. Following America and Britain, Australia had joined the so-called Coalition of the Willing and invaded Iraq, a country he had always wanted to visit, beginning with Baghdad. Parts of Syria, Libya, Somalia, Yemen broke under the strain. He looked on in dismay at the ruins of Aleppo where he had recently stayed. A complex procession of disasters can be written down easily seated at a desk, within the space of a few minutes. Many people were shown fleeing these countries, as well as Afghanistan and Iran, crossing the Mediterranean or taking remarkable voyages all the way to the coast of Western Australia. Officially, at least a thousand people had drowned trying to reach Australia. To stop the boats the government placed all arrivals in camps, mostly on two islands, where, it was declared, they would never leave. The boats stopped. It was cruelty to a few to reduce a larger cruelty, and was disliked by virtually everybody. He was not comfortable with it either, but had not heard of nor could he himself think of a better solution.

If Alexander Pope, known to have been irritable, could say, 'For forms of government let fools contest', and turn his head from the events of the day and produce without doing anyone any harm a body of work highly valued and studied to this day—it is surely better than someone else absorbed in politics and following the daily political news, without making a difference.

As each book was published he met more writers and others involved in publishing. Mostly he liked the way fellow writers thought and spoke. He enjoyed their company. At the same time he didn't wish to be seen entirely as a writer. This unnecessary awkwardness became a disadvantage. Writers were expected to speak in public. Strangers wrote letters, and some included photographs. Reading groups sent questionnaires. There were invitations to festivals, and publishers were keen on interviews. He was asked to write about subjects of which he had little knowledge. Being married to a writer and living together in an apartment became demanding, each one busily guarding their individuality and routines, not wanting to be diminished. The way they each worked was completely different. They held different views of literature. That alone would not be the cause of their difficulties. She was lovely in different ways and wonderfully alert. Despite her response to any suggestion being invariably 'Sure', a certain bleakness grew between them, which alarmed him but was not spoken about. He assumed feminism had given her an independence and edge, enough to handle a separation, and by the time he saw this was far from the case it was too late.

Elusive are the signs of change, the lines which have formed on his face, the way flood-marks are left on walls and trees, most noticeably between the eyes and travelling down one cheek, whether these are not lines but signs left by his doubts and disappointments, the hospitals, broken marriages, the need for money, misunderstandings, a certain abrupt manner, the increasing number of deaths close by, frowning for the truth but usually missing it, the morning in the leper colony, India, his scepticism, eye strain from his working, reading, amounts of wine and spirits enjoyed, the smiles and laughter, plenty of smiles, the exposure to bright light and rain. Various lines can be seen in the mirror, but not what has made them into signs. A set of lines or even a single line would be formed by a combination of events. What he has seen, or suffered, or considered have been the beginnings of marks, yet it is difficult to be sure of what can be revealed by a face. 'All lines of experience are prescribed without your realising it.' The mirror is for shaving, it only takes a minute. At least he has most of his hair, and still fairly thick. White has entered his eyebrows. Of greater concern—his ears appear to have grown larger! He has noticed he has become slightly bent, the years of not holding back his shoulders and standing up straight. He dislikes being photographed and agrees to it only with awkward bad grace; such a reaction he accepts as another form of vanity.

Some people manage to accumulate very few lines. The face of one he knows who is well into his eighties is as smooth as a billiard ball, enough to raise the question of genetics, or what exactly had happened in his life. A smooth life could leave a smooth face. As far as he knows he looks like nobody else on earth. He sometimes imagines another person living somewhere, perhaps in South America, who had exactly the same face, or was so similar as to be alarming should they ever meet face to face. The idea of someone else having his face was too much to think about.

'Stop me if I've told you this!'

It was when a woman left her cigarette on the ashtray for the man to reach over and stub it out for her. Craven 'A's with the red packet. *They never vary.* They stopped making them years ago. And the box of matches had a drawing of a stag's head with antlers on it. At the showground, leaning over the rail following the bony expressionless man driving a 'dodgem car', spinning the steering wheel with one hand, his other arm draped along the back of the seat holding a cigarette, wherever possible turning one-handed to collide into cars being driven by hysterical young women. The cars had masts brushing against an electrified ceiling. When the power was switched off people stepped out of the cars, the girls leaning against each other weak with laughter, while he remained seated, waiting to do it all over again. The artist who carefully illustrated the stag's head for the matchbox and the copywriter who dreamed up the Craven 'A' slogan are both no longer here. Men took a comb if they went out, placing it in their lapel or hip pocket. And so they pulled out the comb wherever they were and smartened up their hair. It doesn't happen anymore. In the green trunk in the garage they found a pile of boomerangs from when their father worked on the cattle station. They tried throwing one or two on the front lawn. He then went around to the back of the house and sent one over the roof where waiting on the lawn in a crouching position was the boy from across the street, who would later have a successful career as an ear, nose and throat specialist. By the time it was dark they had lost most of the boomerangs in hedges and trees or on the street. It was a small excitement—spontaneous and manufactured—to take the mind off the silence of the street. He was about thirteen or fourteen. Looking back, it could be said a certain symbolism had been enacted.

He cannot recall seeing an Aboriginal man or woman while growing up in Adelaide. Only later at Tibooburra and on outback stations did they appear, and averted his gaze.

Hotel in Berlin. Solemn manner and face in shadow of the Greek woman on the pillow.

With her in the bumpy train. What seems to be a natural act made inconvenient.

From the road the crowded mass of legs of the flamingos appeared as a pink stain coming up from the salt pan, Jamnagar in western Gujarat.

Although he has not stepped aboard another container ship he constantly returns to them and surveys the immensity of the sea, the ships themselves large and strong laboured to make headway across the water. In the middle of the ocean the question often arose of how and why such a large part of the world was filled with liquid, and on land there were animals and trees. Flying fish kept up alongside, flashing in the sunlight. On the last voyage in the ship painted matt orange he read again the essays of Montaigne (scepticism, blended with extreme tolerance). The banging, creaking and vibration in the Southern Ocean as enormous black waves came at the ship in threes, damaging it, followed by the long and pleasant conversations on the bridge with the German captain who could speak Mandarin. Tall thin man with a happy face. He described the big seas he had experienced, typhoon in Tokyo Bay in the midst of other retreating ships, a hurricane in the Atlantic where he lost containers, a terrible nuisance 'because of the paperwork'. He lived in a small town in Bavaria well away from the sea. When he returned home after more than four months away he said he had to get to know his wife all over again. Whales, parallel to the ship, going south in the opposite direction, off Western Australia. The incomprehensibility of everything, of light and darkness, of water, everything invisible and felt, his sense of being alive, all impossible to explain. In answer to a question on the bridge the Third Officer who was small and modest said his father during the war had the contract to supply the frames for portraits of Hitler to be hung across Germany in the town halls, post offices and concert halls.

Many crudities, well understood: 'I wouldn't piss on him if he was on fire.'

Looking across the harbour at the golden light

reflected on the glass of the buildings and the feeling of contentment, of happiness even. A long distance from everywhere else. The fact of isolation is not always accompanied by frustration. As shown in other parts of the earth far more extreme cases of isolation are simply accepted.

This particular life: was he allowing it to shape itself entirely, or should he keep providing experiences to bolster an imagined shape? The green bus on the way back from Delphi which began falling apart inside: the ashtray on the seat in front of them fell off, the seat itself holding a silver-haired American broke away and moved along with his protests into the aisle, at the same time the sun visor above the driver slipped down raining maps and business cards onto his head—he had to swat them away like flies; all the passengers laughing, the driver merely shrugging. On the blue-grey ocean the shadows of clouds lay on the water like patches of oil. From the white pillow she opened her eyes in the morning and smiled at the familiarity of him. Earth tremors in Tokyo, Mexico City. In Tokyo the rattle of wooden buildings and a small blue fish flung out of its tank onto the floor where he was staying. Mozart's unfinished Requiem in the church in Vienna, which simply stops, the way *The Man without Qualities* stops, and no less impressive for it, the anxious baritone standing in the front row wearing a dark raincoat actually had the most powerful, moving voice. Amazed at her losing her temper on Bourke Street and not caring about the people passing by. The wrench of the steering wheel as he crashed into other cars, Adelaide. Sightings of flying saucers appeared in clusters and were reported in newspapers, one sighting producing others, which only increased his father's scepticism, while he and his friends were hoping to spot at least one and photograph it. The instinct for a man is to discuss his wife as little as possible. Bougainvillea on the ochre walls in Mexico. Those pigeons kept shifting in formation above his street in Adelaide. Horses were ridden past the open window of the restaurant at barely arm's length away, Avignon; for some mysterious reason it made them happier. Her way of handling a shock was to pour a vodka and sit by herself at the table. The overweight Cuban hairdresser in New York who came back from the lavatory and continued cutting without washing his hands. For driving and looking at films he was prescribed spectacles in London. 'They're not as good as eyes,' said the man at the bus stop. Climbed Mt Kosciuszko with sore ribs and suddenly aware of the cold air. 'It says here, "marriage dissolved"—sounds like acid.' The stories of John Cheever. The blue of the lake at Mount Gambier when he was a boy. Often he laughed at an inappropriate time. Two tall brown horses rushing towards him as he entered their paddock near Braidwood reminding him of the lions at the wire fence outside Harare. Standing in view of her bedroom, Auckland, her expression of expectation which he saw and almost took the one step forward but did not. So accustomed to rain they'd never seen an umbrella. The splendour and yet the ordinariness of sunrises and sunsets, sunrises especially—for their shining optimism. How hot was it in the Sahara—fifty degrees? Approaching to land in turbulence on Gibraltar the alarm shown by the cabin crew when the pilot suddenly aborted. 'Your heart is worn out,' February 26, 2020. Prisoner in Kabul being led along the street in chains. Surprising how noisy a single tree could be—wind in a ghost gum, Flinders Ranges. Smooth rocks in the dried-out creek bed. Thinking it would cover most situations he had begun to say, 'Ha,' or 'Ah-ha!', or 'Yes, I see…'

Admiring the natural world—the animals, landscape modest or extreme, the changing weather—placed him in proportion to the larger order of things. And seeing himself as a small part of it gave him pleasure.

Naturally an unwanted personal experience has a greater force than a remote, more public disaster. Her visits to the oncologists were sudden and the results not good, an operation was arranged quickly. On the train going to the same hospital at Kogarah a man—almost bald, wide face—suddenly began telling him of his wife who had a cancer, 'very bad example of it' and was being operated on 'as we speak', while they were seated together. 'I don't know what I'll do if it doesn't work out. Our son and daughter are no use.' The short walk from the railway station. She had become a horizontal figure. A dazed paleness formed between them, lessened only when they turned to practical matters.

She fell headfirst down from the top of the escalators at Central Railway Station, he alongside unable to prevent it. The escalator was stopped. She was lifted and carried down. The amount of blood and the shock, the obviousness of how a life and lives can be altered in an instant was not at all obvious at the time.

In his early teens he looked up to older men, impressed and interested in their greater experience. Even though with their worn faces and distant expressions they spoke down to him, aware of their position.

Of the many thousands of people he has met and spoken to, and even came to know, almost all are no longer remembered, not their faces, their voices, their manner in general. Already they have disappeared. Their names have loosened and gone away. It is arbitrary. The images of his grandparents, uncles and aunts, and his two brothers and solitary sister, advance and recede. 'Don't you just hate doing up buttons?' Many of those he had known as friends are no longer pictured at all. Some who have died are remembered more than those still alive. A small number are remembered more than others. These appear to be people who have exceptional generosity, or with personality disorders, tricky people, and the infectious optimists, their antics, or those he needlessly offended, women he has hurt. She was into alternative medicines, alternative virtually everything, and had a zany-aunt appearance in unusual colours and short hair. She wanted to be a poet, an actress, a novelist, and attended a clown workshop. She was all kindness and consideration, which was rewarded as she was dying by being portrayed in a book, where her harmless foolishness was pitied and scorned. Away from a mirror he has trouble picturing his own face. Her mother looked like an angry duck, her father like a frog. Strangely, images come forward of figures he has never spoken to. The woman and her husband sitting opposite on the bus from Marrakesh, he elegant in a pale blue robe with an ornamental dagger, she in white with gold trim. Perhaps they were going to a wedding. All he could do was stare at the woman's large dark eyes, gazing back at him while remaining impassive. He couldn't take his eyes off her eyes, the rest of her face hidden behind the yashmak. He tried to estimate her age—early thirties. She had firmly manicured eyebrows. Eventually she offered him an orange, without saying a word. Broad-chested policeman with the army moustache directing traffic at always the same intersection in Adelaide, woman in a butcher shop, Rozelle, whose chin and cheek had a twist as noticeable as any woman's face in a Matisse, so much so he wanted to speak to her and know more.

Events of no consequence or people of only slight

interest appear to prompt other entirely different images. The Goan in the office in Bombay with the mottled face who would sit down and offer advice. On hot days patches of asphalt on the streets melted and became glossy, which no longer happens. Otherwise she was a piece of litmus, registering everything, difficult to live with. To catch tadpoles use a net made from mosquito netting. In summer the coil of adhesive yellow paper hanging from the ceiling in the kitchen to trap the flies. At the screening of *Shoah* at the Jewish Film Festival, Sydney, the elderly man seated alongside told him the Holocaust would not exterminate the Jews. 'A heavy pruning strengthens a tree,' he said in a clear voice. A ballpoint was clipped to his patterned shirt pocket. He had begun with a dry-cleaning business and opened more, 'very successful it has been'.

Often turns into the corner in Dar es Salaam, mid-afternoon, when women and children with startled expressions came rushing towards him away from the old Volkswagen in the middle of the street, which had caught alight, just a few flames from the engine at the back. In an outburst of frustration it was being stoned by young men and a large older woman picking up rocks and sticks and sheets of cardboard, throwing anything at hand, not at the small, patient flames at the back but at the car itself. He wrote a brief essay about it, choosing the title 'Killing an Elephant'.

The new friends he made in Sydney and Melbourne, as old friends in London became closer.

To cover his lack of knowledge of a subject he began to say after making a statement, 'In my opinion…', or sometimes, 'In my humble opinion…'

Delacroix was meaning painting and literature when he said, 'Real superiority…admits no eccentricity.'

Stepping aside from a puddle he usually thinks of the condemned man, as observed by George Orwell in Burma, who does the same thing while being led to the gallows. Why avoid getting a shoe wet when in a few seconds he would be no longer alive? It is all the more moving for showing ordinary behaviour continuing at that final moment. It is this movement of the foot which remains when the rest of Orwell's essay has been forgotten.

She tucked a small handkerchief or tissue up her sleeve at the wrist, a curiously attractive habit taken from the 1950s, now rarely seen.

The early-morning mist rising like a snake leaving the valley, Gundaroo.

A corrugated-iron church, more like a shearing shed, the brown horse standing near the entrance, out of the wind. Near Oberon.

Memory of pain is a poor imitation of pain itself. With the recalcitrant kidney stone, holding onto a lamppost on the street in view of the Colosseum, waving for a taxi to the hospital, which was an old building on the island in the river. More painful still than the broken ribs, Melbourne, was the swollen shin after he fell down the steps, Macleay Street. Resting his hand on a tree in Zimbabwe it was bitten by a hornet. If pain is experience it doesn't add much of quality. It diminishes the body, wiping out areas such as concentration, eyesight and free movement, all of which should function to make up the whole.

And there was always the possibility his faults had contributed to the lines on his face and the expression formed. Especially from the sides of his mouth down to his chin the flesh has loosened, a groove has established, which has him looking grim, when he believes he is not grim at all. He was categorical and did his best to reduce it. There were surely traces left over from moments of turbulence. It was becoming a tired face, certainly marked by events which would not have happened to someone young.

The little house with red bricks the colour of lamb chops. Can see the house, not the street.

In his journals Stendhal recorded being with Napoleon's officer group as they reached Moscow, and as they looked down from their horses at the wooden city it began burning, set alight by the Russians, at which point Stendhal described his toothache. He noted too an early drop in temperature. By all accounts Stendhal behaved well during the retreat in winter from Moscow, which left him as a man of experience. When he met Goethe it was of course all Goethe wanted to talk about.

The pose of irritability spread into actual irritability.

Away from a mirror he had trouble seeing his face.

As a background the skyline of Sydney kept dismantling and reassembling itself. The buildings were constructed of temporary materials and could be replaced after twenty or thirty years with larger, taller blocks featuring the latest architectural fashion, throwing enormous shadows in winter and producing disagreeable winds. In this way it resembled American cities made of impermanent materials, Chicago and Manhattan. Older cities of stone throughout Europe were more resistant of change. The way Sydney has been brutalised by freeways and monorails dividing the foreground, the tunnels for cars, advertising messages on every other surface, some lit up in neon, not allowing the eyes to rest, the utilitarian ugliness of railway stations below ground, and a revolving restaurant in imitation of every other big city. Always a building coming down, a new and for the moment more attractive one going up. It may well have encouraged the dismantling of marriages.

He remained mostly in Sydney. Plenty of others had travelled the world in greater difficulty and farther and more than he had. He couldn't think of anybody who had not been away. If he went anywhere now it was by suburban train or bus, and his walk early in the morning, no more trips to West Africa and such places. Music occupied his spare time more than looking at pictures. He no longer read art books cover to cover or catalogues; or very few. The eagerness for music, chamber music and concertos, had been passed on by his former wife, an infectious disease.

To make himself into somebody measured, who remains at arm's length. Instead he talks readily, is casual with facts (to avoid pedantism) which has him inconsistent, while wanting to be aloof.

At the hospice in Darlinghurst on Tuesday evenings the heightened sense of being alive and moving freely as he attended to figures lying in rows or singly in rooms, each one with little time to live, some would be dying within days. Faint sounds of traffic outside. Some read poetry, some listened to the radio. Others were on the telephone. A few had no visitors and didn't seem at all concerned. Occasionally he was asked to go out and buy cigarettes. Rarely did a patient show signs of fear or bitterness: a Japanese woman of barely forty kept pacing with her arms folded unable to remain in bed and would not talk to anyone, the man who said he helped design the Leyland car—he showed fear of dying in his face and the way he spoke. Was it weakness, or what? A few had been there for a month or more and his regular visits established a familiarity. They could talk more easily to an anonymous visitor than to their families. A healthy black-and-white cat wandered along the corridors, jumping onto beds, presenting to a patient a touch of life from the outside, especially to those who had left an animal at home. She told him with a matter-of-fact shrug she had sold Matisse flowers from her father's shop in Nice; small woman with exceptionally wide mouth. And vegetables—he also wanted aubergines. The husband and wife, in separate rooms; she hadn't been told he too had been admitted with cancer. When he visited her from a ward on the same floor he took care to wear a jacket and tie over his pyjamas. A man with a neck broken from bone cancer unable to move said he never wanted ever to see again the painting on the wall facing him. It was a reproduction of trees in winter by Cézanne. Different approaches to dying, which always ended the same. The anxiety of those being fed with a quickly tilted spoon, not wanting to choke. Whether he was given a special view of life working at the hospice, or that it had any effect at all, he could hardly tell. And he could never say why he had decided to spend time in that place. It was austerity—it had to do with austerity. Returning home later in the evening he would feel unusually tired, at the same time pleased to be back out on the street.

Hard to avoid was the procession of new prime ministers and the behaviour of the deposed ones, six in almost as many years. They passed before us on the screen and in newsprint and lengthy explanations were given on the radio. Of small consolation was the rest of the world appeared little better, in some places far worse. Almost every day Jeremy Corbyn and Boris Johnson were shown turning Britain inward, and extreme figures such as the American president, a law unto himself, making parts of his country happy and the rest of the world very unhappy. China, North Korea, Russia, Turkey, Hungary, Venezuela and others had strong leaders who managed to impose themselves on their own people, which might have appeared to be the easiest way to govern. These figures kept moving about in the background, coming forward with an insistence, keen to be governing or to be noticed, soon enough replaced by another situation, different beliefs, a fresh lot of vaguely familiar faces. Friends with stronger political interests than his would at intervals pronounce words, such as 'Tories' or 'Trump', 'Right Wing' or 'Left Wing' and other reductions, as a way of flagging their own credentials. He was more interested, if only slightly, in the reasons behind a result, and it exasperated him that opinions were reduced to Labor versus the rest, expect nothing worthwhile on the conservative side, vice versa, or if a person was for Brexit they were considered ignorant and to be shunned, and that was the beginning and the end of it, nothing for discussion. Meanwhile he tried to appear balanced and wise by remaining more or less in the middle. But as soon as the single-syllable 'Trump' entered a conversation, as it often did, it produced in him simultaneous irritation and boredom, for the conversation immediately fell into a heap, little new or worthwhile could be added, enough for him to wonder why the world continued to gaze across to America, a country where ordinary social services and laws taken for granted anywhere else were anything but satisfactory, a shambles of individualism, an amazingly poor example, inflicting difficulties on its citizens, while at the same time continuing to intervene in the governing of other countries. Still we looked across to America in a sort of dazed fixation. Mrs Merkel and M. Macron were rarely mentioned, nor were the calmly governed Scandinavian states. He noticed that businesspeople tended to view Britain and Europe with disdain. America had a practical freshness and way of doing business.

Asked what quality is most required of a leader, Mitterrand said: 'Indifference'.

Looking over the bridge at the river flowing through the middle of Geneva: it was the unexpected rush of deep green that left him remembering it.

Various blood thinners taken daily have left him sensitive to cold, unlike in Moscow, winter 1974, when skidding around on the ice in only a raincoat and no gloves he was hardly aware of it being ten degrees below. The slightest bump leaves a bruise. Aside from taking care going down stairs another sign was the way he paused over a situation, and was less afraid of doubts. He no longer minded friends becoming former friends. His right hand began shaking when holding a spoon or filling a glass and had to be rescued by the other hand. Instead of speaking straightaway he would think again. Inability to recall a name had become an embarrassment. And there was his interest in the weather, looks like rain, another hot day. 'What was it yesterday?'—joining in the conversation. Someone liked to point to the 'wind-chill factor'. Then he wouldn't say a word about the weather for weeks on end.

They wore long brown boots, thick knitted pullovers, and happily spoke about wood-burning stoves.

Where was it he saw—but can no longer remember—the fat woman in the floral bathing costume in the motel swimming pool late in the afternoon, banging her arms and grimacing, like a wrestler pinned to the mat? And she had her own existence, her own experience which had the desperate appearance of floundering.

At night the surf was like a large tree crashing down with a whoosh and a thumping in a forest of ferns, Lorne.

It is almost impossible to live without vanity. You are here briefly. Have you tried looking down, as if above the streets and crowds?

Everything he did was difficult. Writing, reading, talking, not talking, walking, remembering, telephoning, loving. Often too indignant.

Meeting older men who had a certain power from success he would immediately become gauche or flippant, without meaning to be.

'Looking forward was happiness—that's all—nothing more.' —Conrad, *Under Western Eyes.*

His experiences made him different from every other person, but not much different. Had it given him a clearer view of people or events—or of himself? After going hopefully into difficult situations in distant places had he acquired extra worldliness—extra anything? Can he now withstand severe misfortune, for example? It felt more as if the inevitable progress of time along with the contemplation of the writings of others had been the main influences. Many more people preferred to remain in the one spot and enjoy the settled life, avoiding losing their jobs and wives, avoiding unnecessary difficulty, modest and useful, family lives, decent, with no need to read the words of others. 'It all begins and ends with love,' she said, more senior than him. Hardly a year later at her flat in London she had been asleep after smoking in bed when it all caught fire. At intervals he thought it very strange his mother and father had allowed him to be and continue to exist.

A landscape as if dusted with flour, the hollows thick, other parts thin, which he can recall more than the cold. Yorkshire, a possibility. It could have been somewhere in Germany, passing from a train. The northern part of the world, definitely.

Unexpected phrases remain: 'He imported a wife from South America.'

On the streets the reduced number of people gave the cities and towns the appearance of an afternoon in the Fifties when there was hardly any traffic. In Adelaide men could step out onto the middle of Magill Road hands in pockets to see if a tram was on its way. At any given moment along its route there might be half a dozen men standing in the middle of empty roads, waiting for a glimpse of a tram. Some who wanted to be ostentatious would spend five minutes or more out in the middle, squinting. Nothing remains of the faces of these men or even the colour of their clothes. And hardly any of them had ever left Adelaide, although some had been to a war. His younger brother's hair was noticeably paler than his. Only a few people could afford to buy a car, so others went about on a motorbike and sidecar, the rider wearing goggles. Now with the lockdown to prevent the spread of the coronavirus, August 2020, and snow at Wilpena Pound, people in Sydney and other cities were instructed to stay indoors, emptying the streets of movement, a great emptiness in broad daylight as if everyone had already died. Pigeons again. A greater distance opened up between people and objects. International and domestic travel came to a halt, which turned the clock back to when airfares were far out of reach and people stayed at home. There was not as much movement on the streets or in the sky. There was less noise on the streets. Skies all over the world had become clear of invisible, dangerous fumes. At home people apparently read more books. Buildings were not as high as now. And since the cafes and restaurants had been forced to close, and no-one could sit at a pavement table and enjoy a small cup of coffee, a habit which had transformed everyday life in the cities and country towns, it too returned to the time when everybody appeared to move in slow motion, drank tea from a pot and ate their meals behind closed doors. As the supermarkets emptied of essential items, spaghetti, tinned soup and bottled water, he recalled the few products spaced out on the shelves at Mr Townsend's corner shop before the onslaught of the supermarkets. Certain memories appear once and never again. A pause in the flow of memories leaves a gap reminiscent of a street empty of traffic, and can remain empty for hours, even days. The many different men and women and the faces attached to them have disappeared, leaving no trace. People nodded when he stepped to one side on a pavement. In further imitation of those earlier less populated days, pedestrians concentrating on keeping their distance in metres not yards acknowledged each other, 'Good morning!'

In whitish light, blurry when figures appear, virtually no colour.

At least that is how he can remember the years, a more or less motionless series of times.